When I Opened My Eyes

Library of Congress Registration Number: TXu001948313/2015-12-26
ISBN-13: 978-1500839888
ISBN-10: 1500839884

Photo Provided by: Ms. L. Smith

Please Note: The names of the characters have been changed to protect the privacy of
individuals

<u>DEDICATION</u>

This book is dedicated to all those who believed in and encouraged me to embark on this journey. In this composition, I have chosen to share my marital experiences with others as a testament that no matter how dark things may seem, no matter how hard it gets, hold on, God is still God. It is through our faith in him and perseverance, that we can be victorious.

ACKNOWLEDGEMENTS

First and foremost, to my beautiful children and grandchildren, thank you for being my reasons to live and press on. I love you more than life itself. To my mother, my siblings, grandmother, aunts and cousins, thank you for loving me even on the days where it was hard to do and for all of your support emotionally, physically and financially, I thank you. To my "Girls", Micki, Keeshea, Tracy, Deanie, Pam F. and Janella, you are more like sisters and I thank you for over 30 years of friendship and love, and for being in the trenches with me. To Kristin, you are one of the most courageous women I know. Thank you for your strength and generosity. To Pam M., and Deanie for giving me food and shelter when I could not provide for myself. And to Quincy and Al, for your unselfish love, I thank you. Ms. Edith, for being my voice of reason and one of my biggest cheerleaders, thank you. To Dana, I cannot thank you enough for your kind

2

words and spiritual support over the years. A special thanks to Jessica R., my "road dog." You already know how I feel and what we have been through. We laugh, we fight, and we cry, but you always have my back. I love you more than you will ever know, and I thank you from the bottom of my heart. To Richandra, I sincerely thank you for all your input, feedback and dedication on this project, you rock! To Latosha S., Tracy B. and Michelle B., for your unselfish love and contributions, I will be forever grateful. To all the people who have prayed (and continue to do so) for me, and shown me love and kindness, I thank you and I love each and every one of you. A very special acknowledgement to *Baby Red*. You were the very first person to ever say to me, "Girl, you should write a book." It was your voice I heard first when I decided to embark on this journey. You were my very first inspiration. Thank you. Most of all, thank you God for all of my trials and tribulations, and for all of your many blessings, for the struggles and the victories.

Thank you, Lord, for your loving kindness and tender mercies, for without you, I truly would be nothing.

<u>INTRODUCTION</u>

I was recently asked if I had to choose, what single word would I use to describe myself? Now initially, I said the word I'd choose would be perfectionist, but, after pondering the thought over a few days; I changed my mind and instead settled on the word, realist; which will help you to understand my next statement. I will not apologize for what I say or how I tell this story; for you see, I was not always trying to live the life or walk in the way of Christ when certain events occurred. However, at the time of this writing, I was striving to do so daily; and this composition is a depiction of my journey. But even as I write this, what I want those of you who are not following Christ to understand, is that, those of us who profess to be Christians, are human and we are *not* perfect. Our feelings and experiences are real. And for those of us who are trying to be Christ like, we need to keep it real, for the world is watching. We mess up, and it's ok to say so, but we must merely keep trying with as much diligence as humanly possible; which is why I have chosen to write this story, inspired by real feelings, experiences, and actions. And while it is not my intent to offend, harm or upset anyone, I will however, relay the events that took place as they unfolded, so that the realness of those experiences is not lost. In doing so, this writing may include verbiage or the indication thereof, that is not considered *"Christ Like"*. Therefore, it is not intended for the faint at heart. Nor is it geared specifically towards those who identify themselves as Christians, but for those who find themselves struggling to find their way. So, no, every sentence does not end with "Thank you Jesus" or "Amen", and if that's what you're expecting, you will not find it here. Does that mean I am any less a child of God? No. It simply means I am human and as a child of God, I may have some growing to do. But hey, didn't the disciples? I mean Jesus' crew consisted of former thugs: murderers, thieves, hustlers and gangsters. Judas betrayed him, Peter denied him, and Thomas doubted him. Yes, real people like me, broken and flawed. There is no perfect Christian. So raw, uncut, and somewhat uncensored, this is my story...

When I Opened my Eyes

Who is this staring back at me?

How did I get here, how can this be?

Looking in the mirror, through the tears,

I don't recognize my own face,

It's dark and lonely, in this place.

What is this I'm feeling, what's happened to me?

I must wake up, shake it off, set myself free.

When I opened my eyes, I could not see...

=

CHAPTER ONE
Jordan: What was I Thinking?

Like most, if not all little girls growing up, I, too, wanted what was referred to as the "perfect life." And while that did not necessarily include the white, picket fence, I did want the attractive, successful husband, along with two point five kids (whatever that means). A handsome son who would be our first-born, followed by a beautiful little girl, and of course a nice home. But little did I know, life would not be perfect. I was raised in a home that was less than perfect and at times unbearable. My own parents divorced when I was ten. However, my dreams and fantasies were not shaken, and I would carry them with me for many years to come.

At the tender age of sixteen, and after many years of sexual abuse, I became pregnant with my first child. The father of my unborn baby and I parted ways shortly after conception, and it was during this time that I met Harold.

Harold was about three years older than I. He was single, childless, in the Marine Corps, good-looking, and of course, I was in love. Although I was carrying someone else's child at the time, he didn't mind, or so he said. He claimed to love me as much as I loved him. We often talked about spending our lives together and I was elated. I had found my prince and all my dreams were about to come true. Or so I thought. And then, my world came crashing down!

One day while thumbing through some photos that belonged to a "good friend" of mine, I stumbled across a picture of her sister (who was also supposed to be my friend) and Harold in a very intimate pose. I was devastated! At that moment, it became very clear to me why, in the weeks prior to this discovery, Harold had abruptly stopped calling and I hadn't seen him much during that time either.

He was now sleeping with her!

My friend, who claimed to love me. The very same friend who had taught me to drive a stick shift, and with whom I had hung-out with daily and at whose house I had spent many nights. This was the same friend who now claimed to love my new born baby and the same friend who would take me to the base on weekends to see my man when she went to visit her own. I considered her family, my family. Yes, we were just that close and had been for years. I was crushed. Through it all, and in the aftermath, I got over the initial shock. I eventually stopped crying and somehow managed to pick up the pieces of my broken heart. All the while, still holding on to that dream. You know the one, "The Perfect Life?" Right.

Over the next four years, I would experience many relationships. The men were usually slightly older and almost always in the military, almost. So, it would stand to reason, that one day, I'd become a military wife. And why not? A guaranteed paycheck, benefits and status. However, this was not the case; at least not at this stage of my life.

At the age of twenty, I was introduced to a young man named Jordan, who would later become my first husband. Our introduction came by way of another young man who was dating my best friend at the time and who happened to be Jordan's childhood buddy. After many phone conversations over several months, Jordan and I developed feelings for one another, and although I lived in California and he lived in Ohio, we began a long-distance relationship. In October of that same year, I left my three-and-a-half-year-old daughter home with my mother and headed to Cleveland, Ohio, to meet my new love face to face, for the very first time. The year was 1986.

As you can tell; we wasted no time and decided

rather quickly, and carelessly I might add, that we were made for each other. Did it matter to me that I had been told he resembled Eddie Murphy when he actually looked like one of the chipmunks? Or that he had been in some minor trouble with the law? No. Who was I to judge? And what did I know? I was only twenty, and everyone has a past, right? So, in January of the following year, in front of a judge and a friend as a witness, we became husband and wife.

By this time, my new husband and I were living in New Hampshire, and in a few short weeks following the exchanging of our wedding vows, he had to return to Ohio and tend to some legal matters; he was gone for about a week. A few days after his return and while we were showering together one morning, Jordan discovered a little tiny, clear-looking bug on his washcloth. It was also during this time we discovered I was pregnant. Startled at what I had seen and taking note of Jordan's own reaction, I began to question him. I wanted to know what he thought the little parasite was. (Call it women's intuition.) He took one look at the towel and without hesitation and to my own horror said, "It's a crab!" Now I was young, (by this time twenty-one), and maybe a bit naïve, okay naïve to the tenth power, but I had learned enough through sex education classes in school to know, there was only one way to contract this parasite, and I also knew that I had not been with anyone but my husband.

Oh, he tried to come up with all kinds of crazy explanations. First, they must have been left behind by our roommate who shared our shower, "Nasty M.F." is what he said. Then, he must have gotten them from a toilet. How many times have you heard that? Boy, did he really think I was stupid. It wasn't until I let him know in no uncertain terms, that I did not believe him, and that I knew he was lying, did he confess to cheating. We had been married for all of three weeks.

I screamed that he'd better hope like hell that I had not contracted this disease. Thankfully for me, and luckily for him, I had not. As time went on, I forgave him, but our relationship was never the same. Oh, I still loved him, but I surely didn't trust him.

Shortly after this episode and with the impending birth of my second child, I decided I wanted to be at home with my family. We agreed that I'd return to California while he stayed behind in New Hampshire and continued to work. We had been apart for maybe thirty days when Jordan stated that he wanted to come for a visit. He had never been to California and I did miss him, so I saw no harm in it. Boy was I wrong...

One week turned into two, two turned into three, three... well, you get the picture. My husband was having a ball living on the West Coast. After about three weeks of watching him do nothing but party, I confronted him about returning to New Hampshire and returning to work. He confessed that he didn't want to go back; he didn't want to leave me. Sure, I am certain that was the reason. He, like so many others, had been turned out by the California lifestyle. I agreed that he could stay on one condition; he had thirty days to find a job.

By now, we were living with my great-grandparents, and while they didn't seem to mind, I on the other hand, did. You see, for me as a single woman, to live with family was fine, but to have to stay with my family along with my husband simply because he did not have his stuff together, was not going to work. I would not stand for it, not from my man. So, I gave him a time limit. Now, some would probably say it was more like an ultimatum and while that may be true, the point is, he had thirty days to get it together or he had to go, period. Back then, I could be both ruthless and hard. It was my way or the highway. I had learned this behavior over the years and as far as I was concerned, I had already given this man one pass too many. In case you've forgotten about the crab incident; let me take a moment to remind you. Now, I wore the pants and I could be a bigger prick than any man you have ever known.

I don't think we quite made the thirty-day mark, or, maybe we did. It has been a long time, but as I recall, I do think it was somewhere between the thirty-second and the thirty-fifth day, when all hell broke loose and that Negro was still out of work!

A couple of days prior to the big blow up, my husband, who had been out doing who knows what, came home stinking drunk! Not only was I angry, but, ashamed and embarrassed. How dare he come into my family's home in this condition? I was reaching the point where I'd had enough, and to add insult to injury; when I went to check on him (after he had stumbled into our bedroom earlier), he had thrown up!

Now, you are probably thinking that I cleaned up both him and the mess. I mean, isn't that what a loving, caring wife does? Yeah, well, by this point you should know that I was not feeling loving nor caring towards him, so, if that's what you thought, think again.

I guess by now you're also wondering, "Where was her salvation, her forgiveness?" During this time, I wasn't really into God, and by that, I mean, I was attending church, but that's about it. Remember, "A work in progress" and I don't mind telling you that God has been on this assignment for a very, very long time. About a week later and again after Jordan had been hanging out all day, we had a knock-down, drag-out that would finally bring our marriage to an end.

My grandfather, who was a preacher, was in town to deliver a sermon at one of the local churches and I wanted to attend the service. I will never forget, I remember it like it was yesterday. Funny how some things you can remember in great detail, and others you cannot. It was a Friday night; my husband was out and had taken our only car. I had been telling him all week about the upcoming service and that I had planned to attend. Now keep in mind that I was pregnant and hardly left the house, but this was important to me and I really wanted to be there, and he agreed to return home in plenty of time.

Service that night started at 7pm, and yep, you guessed right; it was now 7:30 and there was no sign of Mister. Hell, he could have stayed gone, I just needed the car. Oh, did I mention that this Negro was still out of work and was in violation because he had already missed the deadline that I had set for him to secure employment? You would think that he'd want to act right. Wrong. Black people.

I guess it was around 7:45pm when Jordan decided to show, and I was heated! But unlike Celie in The Color Purple, I wasn't afraid of "Mister." No, in fact, I was more like Miss Sophia. Had he been smart, he would have just stayed gone; he was already late. He should have just done like a teenager who stays out past curfew. They know they're going to be in trouble for being late in the first place, so why rush home? I guess he thought I'd just be happy that he showed up. Wrong again.

Of course, an argument ensued, and somehow, during my ranting and raving, I ended up in the driver's seat of our car, and he, in the passenger's. I still cannot figure out to this day how that happened and the only conclusion I can come to is that, I was trying to leave, and he refused to get out of the car. He was smoking a cigarette, and as I continued to curse him out, he decided, of all things, to purposely blow smoke right in my face. Did I mention I was pregnant? I asked him, no, told him, no, I warned him twice, not to do that again. He must have thought I was bluffing, because when he so boldly, no, defiantly, and disrespectfully, proceeded again to blow smoke in my direction, I let him have it. POW! Right in the very place the smoke was coming from. Oh, did I also fail to mention that I was a fighter? I am sure I don't have to tell you, that I never made it to that service. That night, not only did I put my husband out of the house but insisted that he leave town altogether. IMMEDIATELY! I also let him know that if he refused, I'd alert his probation officer that he was in California without permission. To this day he says no one has ever kicked him out of an entire state! Clearly, he had never met me.

Jordan returned to Cleveland in March, and in April, I discovered that I was carrying twins! Great, here I was about to give birth to not one, but two babies, and no husband.

Five months later, I'd given birth to twin girls and Jordan wanted to reconcile, and for a fleeting moment I actually considered it. "Maybe we should. Nope." It was not worth it, and I would come to know soon enough, that divorcing him was the right thing to do.

It wasn't long after he returned to Cleveland, that I discovered he had been seeing someone else in my hometown. I said to myself, "That explains a lot", but I really didn't care. The end, right? Hardly.

When our daughters were around seven months old, my husband informed me that another woman had given birth to his child! Yeah, this story just keeps getting better, and at this point, there was no chance of reconciliation. You see, I can forgive a lot of things, even perhaps infidelity, hadn't I forgiven him of this act once before? But, when you bring another child by another woman into the picture, a child outside of your marriage, it changes things completely. He was now forever connected to this other woman.

As far as I was concerned, he had committed the ultimate act of betrayal, and not once, but twice! Yes, you heard me, twice. This other woman gave birth to their second child, eleven months following the birth of their first. Now, during all of this, and throughout this whole ordeal, he had the nerve, no, the audacity, to continually profess his love for me. He claimed that I was STILL the only woman he truly loved, the one to which he gave his name. (All the while I am thinking, "Humph, that ain't the only thing you almost gave me.") And if I'd let him, he would come home in a heartbeat.

Was he serious? Was he crazy, or, did he just think I was? Sounds like a scene from the *Love and Hip-Hop*

Atlanta series, doesn't it? Well, I'm not Mimi and he certainly was not Stevie J; and any remote or slight chance of us ever getting back together was, null and void.

We were still married. And while I have never held anything against my former husband's other kids, nor their mother for that matter, I knew I was not, nor could I ever be, one of those wives who would continue to stay in a marriage knowing that my husband had fathered the offspring of another. Don't get me wrong, I am not knocking those women who choose to stay in this type of situation, I just know that I am not one of them. And to be honest, by now I really had no feelings of love left for the man, but he was still my husband, and the father of my children.

Was it resentment? Perhaps. But I think maybe I was just disgusted with it all. Yes, that's it, and at that point I was thinking, "Negro, you can have your name back!" I was done and wanted nothing more to do with this shell of a man. I wanted him out of my life for good. Oh, don't misunderstand, I have never stood in the way of my children having a relationship with their father or their siblings, it was, and still is, their choice, but what I did know was that their father and I would never live again as husband and wife. Although I must admit, it was not all bad, there were a few good times and I did get two beautiful daughters out of the union. Next...

Chapter Two
Malcolm: All That a Woman Could Ask For

How Malcom and I met, hmmm, let's just say, that it was not in the traditional sense. In fact, you may, as others have, frown on it and say that the way we came together was less than admirable, but it was what it was, and our union would go on to become overall, the best male/female, husband and wife relationship I have had thus far. The journey with Malcolm would be the one to get me as close as I would come to my happily ever after, and the hardest part of this book that I was forced to live again. Our relationship was comprised of happiness, love, challenges and heartbreak; but I wouldn't change what we shared for anything this world has to offer, except perhaps, the ending. Like most famous love stories, ours too, would end in tragedy.

My girls (my closest friends since high school) and I were inseparable. We were hanging out at Vista Entertainment

Center, one of the hottest spots in North County San Diego at the time. It was 1989 and the pickings at the Marine Corps Base, Camp Pendleton, were plentiful. The men didn't mind spending their money and it seemed as if every woman was on the prowl to snag one, and vice versa of course. My girlfriends and I would come to know the next few years as a time of partying (usually six nights a week) and hanging out at Buddy Todd Park in Oceanside, California on Sundays.

Exposed brassieres, cat suits and hot pants were in fashion. Yes, hot pants had made a comeback. The musical group Soul II Soul was an all-time favorite with their hit, "Keep On Movin'". It was a time that we here on the West Coast discovered a dance called The Electric Slide. The music was good, there were plenty of men and the party was on. Yep, my girls and I were all in.

It was during one of our many nights of serious (and

I do mean serious) partying, when we were together, and we met Malcolm. Now initially, I was not at all interested in Malcolm. In fact, it was my girl, Latrice, who took a liking to him, and he to her. I actually had another man living with me at the time, but I knew our relationship wasn't going to last. While my man at the time was decent enough; a good provider, not bad on the eyes, and in the military, the fact remained that he was also a nerd, mediocre in bed and somewhat of a coward, which meant that at some point, he would not be able to keep my attention. Unfortunately for him, he became a casualty of my survival hustle; but that's another story.

Now in the beginning, as I mentioned, I had no interest whatsoever in Malcolm. He was dating my girl Latrice, but as time went on, my feelings for Malcolm would change and I could clearly hear some familiar words spoken to me by a woman who was very close to me. During one of our many conversations, I made the statement, "I would never date a man that had dated one of my friends." She turned to look at me and said, "I once said the very same thing to a wise old man, and he said to me, "You haven't seen anything you wanted yet." That woman was my mother and the wise old man, my grandfather. You could have knocked me over with a feather. Never say what you won't do. Now before you pass judgment, let me finish explaining just how we came together.

My girlfriends and I spent alot of time together, as a matter of fact, we did almost everything together. We graduated high school together, we even left our hometown, and all relocated to San Diego County together and during this particular time, we were all living in the same apartment complex. Now, some of you might go on later to say that was the problem, we spent too much time together, but we were each other's support, and believe it or not, to this day, we remain the closest of friends. At least, we were at the time of this writing anyway.

I guess some would also go on to say that Latrice's first mistake was the fact that she didn't have a home phone. Now, you might be wondering what this seemingly small detail had to do with anything; keep reading, it gets better. Remember, this was the late eighties and although during this era things were a lot better for most of us, times could still get tough. Cell phones were not the rave they are today and even if they had been, most of us couldn't afford them. So, whenever Malcolm wanted to reach Latrice, he would do so through me. He would call my home and I, being the "good" friend that I was, would either run over to Latrice's and get her, or make sure she got his messages.

Things seemed to be going well between Malcolm and Latrice for a while, and then, the situation became a little...shall I say, complicated? I've already spoken of how much time my friends and I spent together; well, for Latrice and me, that didn't seem to change, even when she started dating Malcolm. It seemed as though I spent just as much time with the two of them as they did with each other. Not good? Some people would probably say this was Latrice's second and most lethal mistake.

At first, I referred to Malcolm as my brother. Ironic, to say the least, but at that time, it was appropriate because he was dating my sister-friend. However, as time went on, he and I grew closer. I honestly wasn't aware of how close we had become until one day, after one of our many sessions of horseplay, (ladies do not let your man play with other females) during which Latrice was always present, I began to notice what seemed like a developing chemistry between us.

Spooked and shaken by what I was feeling, I went home and called Stephanie, another member of the posse.

I was truly trying to rid myself of the emotions that were running through my veins for my friend's man and I figured Stephanie, who always thought herself to be the voice of reason of the group (and usually was), would be just the deterrent I needed. I figured she would tell me to stop tripping and get a grip; boy did I figure wrong. After a brief moment of idle chatter, I confided in her the real reason for my call. I said to her, "If Malcolm doesn't leave me alone, I'm going to sleep with him." And to my surprise, her response was, "Go ahead, Latrice don't want him." I was shocked, initially, but with that, all of the fear and guilt I had been feeling was no longer an issue.

I know, I know, by now you're probably saying to yourself, "Those _____ (you fill in the blank) were not Latrice's friends! But again, let me stop you in your tracks. You see, Latrice had previously confided in our other friends and I that she did not want Malcom, which is probably why

Stephanie responded the way she did. Had Malcolm been someone Latrice was really into or cared for, things would have unfolded quite differently. Couple the statement made by Latrice along with her behavior at the time, and it should have come as no surprise to anyone that it was only a matter of time before things between she and Malcolm would come crashing down. Right or wrong, it was what it was, and it was Latrice's final mistake.

Do not misunderstand, I am in no way trying to make excuses nor justify my actions and I accept full responsibility for the role I played in all of this, but what I am saying is, that she, too, had a part in the demise of the relationship between her and Malcom. I am just relaying things as they happened, and while I will not go into detail of what I know personally about Latrice's behavior and what transpired at the time, I will relay some of the events as told to me, by the man whom would later become my husband. It would be those events that also led up to, and sealed the fate of not only their relationship, but the union of mine and Malcolm's as well.

As far as I was concerned, Latrice was a grown woman, single and free to do as she saw fit. She dated numerous men, hell, we all did. Sometimes, one man at a time, sometimes, many at once, and sometimes, not at all. There was nothing wrong with that. In fact, back in the day it was called courting and it only became a problem when you were the only one in that circle who knew that you were dating more than one person at a time, which was the case with Latrice and Malcolm. And while I cannot or will not say he was totally dedicated to her, what I will say is that I never saw him behave inappropriately, nor had I ever heard about it; not even from Latrice. That is, unless you consider our horsing around, but don't forget, Latrice was always present when that went on. I do, however, have firsthand knowledge about some of the good things he did, because, of course, I was there.

If you recall, Latrice did not have a home phone and well, one day my phone rang, and it was Malcolm on the other end. This was not unusual, and I assumed he was calling for Latrice, but the conversation took a turn for which I was not prepared. He wanted to know who the guy was in the car he had just seen Latrice driving. I almost swallowed my tongue, bit my lip and choked all at the same time. I never saw this coming, and while I would not rat on my girl, I was not going to lie for her either. I merely told him that I had nothing to do with what was going on between them and that he should talk to her. Yep, I had dodged a bullet.

A couple of weeks later, Malcom knocked on my door and he was irate (my man, the nerd, was away at the time). He wanted to know what kind of fool Latrice had taken him for? He went on to explain that, while he was home with her kids one night in her apartment, he knew that she was in the apartment below hers, at our friend Shelia's house, with another man (which she was). He went on to say that the straw that broke the camel's back, was that one day after Latrice had given him a key to her home, he had gone there and let himself in, only to find another man lying across her bed! I had not heard about this incident, and let me reiterate, I did not live in her house and had no firsthand knowledge of this, so I cannot say for certain; these were his words. There was one thing however of which I was certain, and that was the fact that this man was not in my house making a scene for nothing, it really wasn't his nature. He was actually kind of quiet...for the most part.

Shortly after that defining moment, Latrice and the nerd were out, and Malcolm and I began to plan our lives together. Okay, okay, we began dating. I can hear you saying to yourself, "Wait a minute; that was her friend's man, and what happened to the nerd? And how did she know he wouldn't do the same thing to her?" Well, I did not know for certain that he would not do the same thing to me, but I was willing to take that chance. What I did know, was that I was not the only woman or associate of ours who had her eyes on Malcolm. For the most part, we all knew he was a pretty good catch and remember, I was now a single mother trying to survive. I had him in my clutches and I wasn't about to give him up. And in case I failed to mention it, he was in the military, single and had no children; so, yes, my survival instincts kicked in and weighed heavily on my decision. Self-preservation is a powerful thing. I had three kids to raise, and as far as him being my friend's man, she didn't want him. Remember? And I reminded her of that when she approached me about the situation.

Latrice assumed that Malcom and I had been seeing each other behind her back. She said to me, "He was sleeping with you while he was sleeping with me." And my reply, as harsh as it may seem was, "No, he stopped having sex with you, when he started having sex with me." It was the truth. The minute Malcolm and I started having a relationship, they were done; whether she knew it or not. Latrice, of course and understandably, stopped speaking to me. But, it wasn't so much the fact that Malcolm was with another woman, or even another woman of our crew, it was the fact that the other woman happened to be me. Let me explain.

Latrice and I had a bond that was probably closer, at the time, than any of the others in our group, a bond that ties us together for life. You see, her youngest brother is the father of my oldest child. Yes, it's deep, I know, and it is funny how I never stopped to consider how Latrice felt, or maybe I did; for a fleeting moment. I mean, this very thing was done to me many years prior, but just like that, the thought was gone. As for the nerd, a few days later he came back to what was once his home, only to find Malcolm, lying in the space he once occupied. Cold blooded? Yeah, I know.

As time went on, Latrice and I mended our friendship, and eleven months later, on November 29th, 1990, Malcolm and I stopped dating and became husband and wife. We never had a formal wedding, and like every married couple, we had our share of ups and downs, but, despite a few hiccups along the way, our union was one of the best. The good definitely outweighed the bad, and my childhood dream had finally become a reality. Malcolm was my knight in shining armor and I looked forward to spending the rest of my life with him.

You might now be wondering, what made this man so special. Why would I think he was the one for me considering how we met? If there was one thing I knew, it was that this man loved me, and more importantly, he loved my children. He came right in and stepped up to the plate as any real man would. Not only was he a good husband, but also an excellent father to my girls. In fact, he cherished the girls so much that he became irate when, during a conversation, I innocently let one of his superiors know that he was not the girls' biological father. Needless to say, I never made that mistake again. By all accounts, he was their dad, which is probably the most important role he ever played, at least, in my opinion. The way I see it, most people have it backwards. I've heard it said a million times, "Anybody can be a daddy", but I am telling you they cannot. What is true, is that anyone of the male species can be a father. Dogs father puppies, rats father mice, and even boys as young as ten or eleven can father children, but it's a real man, a dad, who goes beyond the physical act of fatherhood. And while Malcolm never physically fathered any children of his own, he was the best daddy my children could have ever had.

He was careful to make sure he could provide for us, sometimes working two or three jobs, and he would do everything in his power to not only fulfill our needs, but also our desires. For me, personally, it was the little things he did that were so special. On any given day, I'd get flowers or a card, just because. Yes, it was those little romantic gestures that I treasured and that I miss the most. Oh, there were times when I wanted something, and he told me no, or put his foot down, but he had me spoiled and eventually, I got what I wanted. He just wanted to see me happy. He was my best friend and we did just about everything together, no matter what it was, good or bad. I can recall a physical confrontation with some of our neighbors. He was on one end of the parking lot fighting and I was on the other end, doing the same. We had each other's back. Yep, Bonnie and Clyde all the way, and as far as I was concerned, ours was truly a union to be admired.

After a year and a half into our marriage, Malcolm decided that the Marine Corps was no longer a place he wanted to be, so upon his discharge, we packed up and moved our family to his hometown of Rahway, New Jersey. While there, we resided with his parents in their home along with Malcolm's two grown brothers, three nephews and a niece. We were literally living on top of each other. There was a total of six adults and seven children all living in an old, two-story, four-bedroom house with only one bathroom! Can you imagine?

At one point, Malcolm's other brother (there was a total of four boys in his family), his wife and their two kids also moved in temporarily. Talk about culture shock! I can only imagine what might have been going through the minds of my three small children who were used to having their own space. They probably thought I'd lost what little mind I had, and it might have gone a little something like this. *"Why did she move us here? Making us give up our room to share attic space with her and dad?"* That's what I would have been thinking, but my husband and I knew that it was only a temporary situation.

We had been in New Jersey just about six months when Malcolm and I had a major blow up. And when I say major, I mean to the point that we would end up separated for six months because of it. Now you might wonder; if overall ours was a good marriage as I previously claimed, why or what could have happened that was so bad we couldn't work it out for six months? Well, I never said our union was perfect. We, too, had our share of problems and had engaged in arguments before, however, during this specific confrontation, my loving husband, the man who my kids had come to know as a doting father, crossed the line. He had hurt one of my children. Don't be alarmed, he had not physically done anything to her. He would never do that. No, he had hurt her emotionally. Let me explain.

Like I said, we had our share of arguments, but I was always careful to keep our kids out of our disagreements, so on this day, when I saw that a serious confrontation was inevitable, I sent the kids upstairs to their room. After what seemed like hours of yelling, screaming and threats, I left the house to make a phone call. I'd had enough of the way we were living and was planning my escape. I returned home to find my husband gone and my oldest child at the bottom of the stairs, crying.

It was the weekend before her birthday and I had purchased a Turbo Grafx 16 Video Game Console she could use on her small television as a birthday gift. When I asked her what was wrong, she turned and looked at me with tears in her eyes and said, "Daddy took my TV, *and* my game." I was horrified, livid and pissed off to the tenth power and, my anger only intensified when she further wanted to know, "Why did daddy do that to me?" Even now, it is difficult for me to write this. The man she had grown to love, adore and respect as her father, her dad, had hurt her in his quest to hurt me! He had overstepped his boundaries, and I was now out for blood!

Nobody, but nobody messes with my kids, PERIOD! Not my mama, not even Jesus! I know, I cannot whip nor, can I control Jesus or what he does, but I use him as an extreme example so that you know just how serious I am. Jesus knows where I'm coming from, and Malcom did too, which explains why he took flight and left the house before I got back. He had opened a can of worms he could not close and he knew I was not the one to be played with, especially when it came to my daughters.

He knew all too well that I didn't just talk, act, nor claim to be a little crazy, I was; especially, when it came to my kids. He had bared witness to this fact on more than one occasion when my anger had been unleashed on others, and had experienced it himself, but only in small doses and never to the level of where things escalated on that night. When that fury rose in me, the devil in hell backed up, I didn't need his assistance!

When Malcolm finally and quietly crept back into the house that night, he slept in his brother's room. I guess he thought his brother could protect him or that he'd have a better chance of going up against me if there were two of them. It's funny to think about it now. My husband was 6'1" and one hundred eighty-five pounds, here I was, all of 4'11", a measly ninety-eight pounds; and he was scared to death! In fact, in the weeks that followed the altercation, he said to me, "I was afraid to stay in my own mama's house." I'm sure you're probably laughing hysterically by now, but, he was right to be afraid. When I got angry, you would have thought I was seven feet tall and had I really wanted to get at him, it would have taken more than he and his brother to stop me. For those of you who don't know, when you mess with a mother's children, her animal instinct kicks in. It is truly like tangling with the devil and you really do not know how you are going to come out of it. Oh, and by the way, I discovered later that night, that his mother had removed all the knives from her kitchen. Smart lady.

The next morning, after my mother and a good friend of mine spent much of the previous night via phone calls trying to calm me down and convince me not hurt Malcolm, I packed up my kids and I left. I had a tank full of gas in the Cadillac that we owned at the time, twenty-five bucks, and a purse full of food stamps when I made my departure. After putting some distance between us and

Rahway, we stopped at a grocer somewhere in Pennsylvania, and with the food stamps, bought food for our journey. I then purchased a road map, and, with the help of my oldest daughter, who was ten at the time, sharp as a tack and who would serve as my co-pilot, planned our route to Memphis, Tennessee, where we had family.

You may be wondering, *"How did they make it all the way to Tennessee on one tank of gas and only twenty-five dollars in their pockets? "* Well, thank God for family and good friends. My mother and my best friend Stephanie, (you remember her) who is also the Godmother to my twin girls, wired us money the whole way until we reached our destination. I cannot say that it wasn't scary being out on the highway with my babies, all alone, especially when, as an adult (except for one other time), I had only traveled cross-country by car with my husband. I wasn't even sure that old car would make it, but I was determined. Yes, my faith was strong, and I knew God would get me and my girls there safely, one way or another.

After being on the highway for what seemed like hours, we'd finally made it to Nashville. It was raining, the water seemed to be coming down in buckets, and visibility was next to zero. It was so bad that even the truckers, who are supposedly better trained than your average driver, had to pull off to the side of the road. So, with some of the money I had collected thus far, I got us a room. God is good. He had given us traveling mercies and held the worst of the storm at bay until my children and I could safely settle in for the night. Even in my mess, God was by my side! (Excuse me for a moment while I get my praise on.)

Shortly after we arrived in Memphis and Malcolm realized that we were gone and not coming back, he was determined to rejoin his family, but at the time, I wasn't so sure that would happen. I just could not get over what he had done, not to mention how hurt my daughter was. It was all so unnecessary. Our argument on the night prior to the kids and me leaving started, ironically, over our car; something simple and stupid. But, it was his behavior (and perhaps my own), that had escalated things. In a nutshell, he wanted the keys to the car and when it became apparent that neither he, nor the police, (he called them on me) could force me to give them up, he flipped! What I didn't mention earlier, is that Malcom's first reaction to my refusal of his request, was to threaten to jump on me. He had never gotten physical with me, nor even threatened to do so, but, when he saw that I wasn't spooked by his threat, and instead quickly grabbed two butchers' knives from a drawer in the kitchen and invited him to "dance," he decided against it. It was after this that I'd left the house and the incident between he and my daughter occurred.

As far as I was concerned, for him and me to argue

over something so petty was one thing, but to put our child in the middle of it, was something else altogether. For that reason, and that reason alone, I had doubts if we could ever reconcile; and if it was possible, I wasn't sure of when. It was not only my feelings or his that I had to consider, but my child's feelings as well. It was November 1992.

At some point, after about four months of separation, Malcolm and I decided we wanted to put our family back together; but once again, it wasn't solely our decision. Now some of you might think we gave our daughter too much control and that a child, (who was now 11) should not have been the deciding party in all of this, but I beg to differ. If you recall, Malcolm was her step-father, and initially, she wanted nothing to do with him. Yes, she did learn to love him when it became apparent that he was going to be in my life and a part of hers, but the adjustment at first was hard for her to get used to.

You see, during the first four, in fact, almost five years of my oldest child's life, it was just her and me. Then for the next two years, and outside of my brief marriage to Jordan, the twins were the only other people who shared our world. So, when Malcolm came along, she was a little resentful towards him and didn't want him around. It took some time, and now, after she had let her guard down and accepted him, after she had learned to love and trust him, he had hurt her. Therefore, the decision to reconcile, was not ours alone. I'd made it painfully clear to my husband that before he could join us in Memphis, before we could be reunited as a family, and although we had forgiven one another for the roles we individually played that led up to the separation, it was the forgiveness of our child that he had to have. He had to regain not only her love, but also her trust. Not only did he agree, but he understood, completely.

While separated, and before it was decided that we would get back together, Malcolm and I both dated other people, but I had no idea what a fatal mistake I had made nor how my decision would come back to haunt me over, and over, and over again. This is where my story gets difficult to relive, and the hardest part to write.

There were approximately four men that I dated during our separation, and only for brief periods of time. But of the four, an affair I had with one man in particular, Damon, would prove to be the most toxic and it would later be revealed that he was the one whom I should have avoided all together.

One day after our short-lived encounter had ended, Damon, who also happened to be my neighbor, and I got into an argument. As I sat on some steps that led to another neighbor's apartment, my feet dangled over the side of the rails and in front of the door that led to Damon's place. He slapped me on the bottom of my feet and ordered me to move them. Crazy, right? It was like this guy had a vendetta against everyone in the neighborhood.

At one point, he threatened to burn down the entire building we all shared, simply because in the weeks prior, none of us wanted anything further to do with him. Yes, he was on one. In fact, on another occasion, when all the kids (mine and my neighbors') were outside playing, he said something off the wall to them. Well, as you already know from previous accounts, no one puts their hands on me, and no one messes with my kids; so of course, me being who I was at the time, I set out to get him. But before I could release my revenge on him, two things happened. First, he apologized for his behavior, and second, during this time, Malcolm went missing.

I had not heard from my husband in over a week. We were still separated, and he was still in New Jersey.

When I finally heard from him, and before he could explain why he had been missing in action, I became upset, and in my tirade, and later to my own detriment, I mentioned the incident with Damon. A slip of the tongue, and naturally, Malcolm became angry. If there was one thing he would not and did not tolerate, it was someone messing with his wife and kids...ironic isn't it? Especially, since it was his actions that ultimately led to our separation in the first place. But you know how it goes, I can mess with my folks, but no one else can.

By now, our oldest daughter had forgiven her dad and it was decided that it was time Malcom joined us in Memphis. He stated that upon his arrival, he would "deal with it," referring to the situation with Damon. I tried to convince him that there was no need. I explained to him that Damon had apologized and that I was just venting, but he refused to listen. I knew my husband well enough to know that he meant just what he said, and that he would, in fact, deal with Damon. It was then that I realized the mistake me and my big mouth had made.

Approximately two weeks later, the girls and I picked up Malcom from the bus station. I don't know who was more excited, he, the kids, or me. I just know that we were happy once again to be a family. But what I didn't know, was, how short lived our time together would be. It was Sunday, the 23rd day of May 1993.

The next two days were wonderful. I took my husband by to meet some of my relatives and just enjoyed watching him and our daughters get reacquainted. The girls were so happy to have their daddy home, and he, no doubt, was glad to be back in their lives. He truly did love them.

On the following Tuesday, we decided to take the girls out for ice cream, but while we were getting ready and before we could leave, there was a knock at the door. It was one of my neighbors; and when I opened the door with Malcolm standing directly behind me, she simply said, "Damon is downstairs." You see, Malcolm had stated in a prior conversation with this woman and her husband (who had become more than just mere neighbors), that he was going to have a talk with Damon, so of course she felt it was her duty to inform us that he was "available." She would later confess to me, how she regretted her decision to come to my home that dreadful day. Once again, I tried in vain to convince my husband to drop it, but he would not hear of it. I went on to tell him how unstable this guy Damon was and that I'd recently learned he carried a razor blade underneath his tongue. My husband's only reply was, "I am not afraid of a razor blade." Malcolm then proceeded to make his way outside and down the stairs, I was right behind him.

When we finally made it outside, a small crowd had

gathered. I mean, people I had never seen before. Some were just hanging out, (it *was* summer), but on this day, there seemed to be more people outside than usual. Maybe it was just my imagination, or even paranoia, but the influx of people, coupled with the fact that Malcolm had in essence put the word out about his intentions, left little room for doubt, that the increase in the outside activity around our home that day, was a mere coincidence. And when I say he had put the word out, don't misunderstand, he was not the kind of man to go around boasting about what he was going to do, he merely told one couple and that was all it took.

When Malcolm approached Damon, he simply wanted to know what Damon's problem was with his family. Now, remember as I stated and inferred in a prior paragraph, that by nature, Malcolm was pretty quiet. Anyone and everyone who knew him would attest to this.

So, unless you were standing within direct earshot of these two guys, (which only the parties involved were), you would have never known there was a confrontation taking place.

After some brief exchanging of words, Damon retrieved his blade from his mouth and armed himself. Malcom also armed himself with a knife I had given him earlier. You didn't think I was going to let him go down there empty handed, did you? Malcolm then said to Damon, "You put yours down, I'll put mine down and we can handle this like two men," meaning a fist fight. When it became apparent that Damon would not comply, Malcolm then turned to me and said, "Go get my s—t!" I understood exactly what he meant. He wanted "Earl," the name he used when referring to his gun. Although I was hesitant to leave his side, I did as I was told and went back upstairs to our apartment to retrieve his weapon. This is where the story takes on an eerie twist.

While I was able to put my hands on his gun rather quickly because he hadn't unpacked yet, to my horror, I discovered it was empty and I could not locate the bullets! I remember thinking to myself, *"Why on earth would he send me to get an empty gun?"* I searched frantically for the missing ammunition, while at the same time, glancing through a window, periodically, trying to keep my eyes on the events taking place outside. Coming up empty handed, I placed the 10MM Colt Delta Elite Pistol, usually filled with hollow point bullets, in my purse and headed back downstairs. When I finally made it back outside, my husband and Damon had parted ways, apparently, without incident.

Malcolm was now standing on the steps in front of our building and Damon was leaning against the vehicle he had been leaning on before any of this began. And while I was not privy to what had been said after my swift departure to retrieve Earl, my husband assured me that everything was fine. Not completely satisfied that all was well, I began to probe Malcolm about the whereabouts of his bullets. He and another neighbor of ours with whom he was speaking at the time, both turned to me and said, "Relax, he don't want to do nothing," and with that, Malcolm then instructed me to take his weapon back upstairs and put it away. Still, I could not shake the uneasiness I was feeling. Call it women's intuition, but in my gut, I knew something wasn't right. I knew this was far from over.

In the next moment, I was certain I'd witnessed Damon snap. He had walked across the street to another apartment unit and when he crossed back over to where we were, he went back to leaning against the same car. As I turned and glanced in his direction, he began to almost violently shake his head from side to side and I felt a cold chill run down my spine. Damon then got off the car, walked towards the back of the apartment complex and disappeared. Upon seeing this, I again questioned my husband about his bullets and tried to relay to him, in vain, my concerns. I pleaded with him to listen to me, to at least arm himself, but, to his own detriment, my words fell upon deaf ears. He chalked up my concerns to being paranoid and told me to chill. (Why are men so hard headed?) Fifteen minutes had gone by, and everything seemed to be okay. Then, things took a turn for the worst.

Malcolm, who was now sitting on the steps that led to our apartment building while I stood directly behind him, continued to engage in conversation with our neighbor. I, on the other hand, wasn't doing much talking. Now, I know those of you who know me personally, may find that hard to believe, but I was too busy visually scanning the surrounding area from time to time. My street senses were on high alert, and I do mean at level orange. I just couldn't shake what I was feeling.

I had briefly rejoined the conversation when Damon reappeared. He had apparently circled the block and was now headed in our direction. As he continued to walk toward us, I couldn't take my eyes off him, and the feeling I had intensified with every step he took. On the other hand, my loving husband, who was a former member of the military police force, a sharp-shooter and trained for battle; was not concerned in the least bit. In that moment I did not know what to make of it all and I began to second-guess myself. Was I tripping? Was Damon coming to make amends, or was he merely walking down the street? My mind raced, and as all these thoughts played out in my head, Damon kept coming. When he was within about ten feet of us, he pulled out a gun...and began shooting!!!

As the shots rang out, Malcolm and I, who were both

64

in the line of fire, ran in opposite directions. I watched, in helpless disbelief, while crouching behind our car as Damon continued to give chase and pursue my husband, all the while, firing his weapon.

It's funny how things can enter your mind at the most inopportune times. I remember saying to myself as I watched this horror unfold right before my eyes, "We live on a slope, our yard is slanted, and Malcolm (who was not accustomed to how the ground was formed and was still recovering from a bullet wound to his leg a couple of years prior), is going to lose his footing!" Just as the thought left my mind, I heard another shot and then nothing...my husband was down! The next few seconds are a bit of a blur and I think I may have blacked out momentarily from the horror that was taking place because, according to my neighbors, after my husband had fallen and was lying face down in the grass, Damon stood over him, aimed his weapon at Malcolm's head, and pulled the trigger once more. This time, however, I was told (and I am sure to Damon's surprise) the gun just clicked. Now, I do not know if it was empty or if it simply jammed, but by now I had come out of my fog and returned to reality, just in time to see Damon flee the scene.

I couldn't grasp what was happening. As my husband lay helplessly on the ground, I knew he was fighting for his life. As I ran to his side, I could see him breathing sporadically. I thought of my children, who no doubt had heard all the commotion and would soon hear the ambulance that was on the way. At that moment there was not a whole lot that I could do for Malcolm, so I headed upstairs.

You are probably wondering how I could leave Malcolm at a time like this, if even just for a moment. But you must understand, the first thing I thought about was damage control! I did not want our children to come outside and witness such a horrible scene, and while there were no visible signs of blood, their father had been shot and was lying face down on the front lawn. After giving the kids a brief rundown of what was happening and assuring them that their father would be okay, I ordered them to stay in the house and I headed back downstairs to be by the side of my man.

As I made my way back outside, I could hear the sirens and I knew help was on the way. I began talking to Malcolm, commanding him to stay with me. Hindsight says, I should have been praying for him and telling him to pray as well, but when something like that happens, believe me, you just cannot think straight. Well, at least, I couldn't.

I stood back as the paramedics made their way over to assist my husband, and after a few minutes, they brought out the gurney. At least he was alive. As they picked up his body and turned him over to place him on the gurney, his arms went limp, and although he was still breathing, I knew then in my heart, he would not make it.

By this time, my cousin, who lived nearby and had heard what went down, made her way to my home and offered to drive me to the hospital. I did not ride in the ambulance because I had to get the kids squared away. So, we dropped them off at her home and then made our way to the hospital. I must tell you that while this chapter is the most beautiful to write, it is also the most difficult, because again, I must relive what happened next...

When my family and I arrived at the hospital, we were instructed to go immediately to a special waiting room. I had never heard of such a thing, but then again, I had never experienced this situation either, so, we did as instructed. As we approached the "special room", I stopped dead (no pun intended) in my tracks. Above the door was a sign, and although this happened over 20 years ago, I can still see it like it was only yesterday. I can only recall the first few words which simply said, "In a time of sorrow..." That's all I remember, because from that point, they had to drag me into the waiting room. My biggest fear, although not yet confirmed by the doctor, was very real. I knew Malcolm was dead, but still, I was holding on to my faith and praying for a different outcome.

The doctor came in about 20 minutes later and said those dreadful words. You know the ones you hear on television, or in the movies? He got as far as "I'm sorry" ... and I screamed. Keep in mind, I already knew in my heart that Malcolm was gone even before the paramedics picked him up, all the signs were there. His sporadic breathing, limp body, the special waiting room; but the confirmation from the doctor made it all too real. I felt like my heart had been physically ripped from my body. All I could think about at that moment was, how could I tell my three small children, who loved Malcolm so much, that their father was gone...again? But this time, he was not coming back.

Once I could compose myself, the doctor explained to me that Malcom had died twice on the way to the hospital, and though they did their best to save him, the bullet had gone into his side and come out through his heart, piercing his Aorta. Now if you know anything at all about the human body, then you know that this vital artery is irreparable, there was really nothing they could do.

I was then allowed to see Malcolm. There was something tugging at me and I just had to see him. To my surprise, it was not the gruesome scene like you see on TV. He was lying in bed and they had taken great pains to clean him up. His body was immaculate. In fact, had it not been for the tube they left in his mouth and the coldness of his body, you would have thought he was just sleeping, however, I knew that this was not the case. I also knew that this would not be the last time I laid eyes on him; it was time to prepare for his funeral.

After I gathered myself together, I made the excruciating ride to my cousin's home to deliver the news to my children. It was May 25th, 1993 and Malcolm was dead. He had only been home for two days. By the time I got there, word of Malcolm's death had already reached my family back in California and the calls had started pouring in. My mother, who loved Malcolm almost as much as she loved her own children, promised to come be by my side; she said she would arrive in a few days. As comforting as it sounded and although I was with my children and extended family, I still felt very alone.

In the days that followed, and as I continued to try and wrap my mind around of how, in just a matter of minutes, my whole life had changed, I knew I had to move on. I had to somehow keep it all together. I went back to the home I had shared briefly with my love to assess the situation. I had not been back to our apartment since the horrific tragedy, and as much as I did not want to, I was forced with the painful task of going through my husband's belongings. I was holding up well, initially, during the process, when I came across a brown paper bag. I touched it and it made an unusual sound. As I proceeded to explore its contents, an uneasy feeling ran through my body and even before I opened it, I knew that the discovery of its contents would make me gasp. I pressed on, and just as I thought and to my realization, my hunch was confirmed, for in this bag I found the bullets for Earl. Once again, I broke down and cried. At that point, I was done going through Malcolm's things.

A few days later, my mother arrived from California. Not only to be by my side, but she would also perform my husband's eulogy, and for this I was truly grateful. Her presence made things a little easier, and when I questioned why it all happened; she was there to give an explanation and words of comfort, which of course, helped to alleviate some of the pain, and most importantly, some of the guilt I was carrying. My children, in their youthful wisdom, were truly a blessing as well. While it was I, who should have been strong for them, they became my strength and they handled the entire situation much better than I did. I can remember, one night when I was crying, my twins, who were only five at the time, turned to me and said, "Don't cry mama, daddy is in a better place." I was floored by the fact that God would use those little children, the people I would least expect, to bring me comfort. *"Train up a child..."* There were others who also came to see about me, but one person in particular was my friend Jackie. Jackie was also from California, but at the time, like me, was residing in Memphis. Jackie was, among other things, my P.I.C. or my partner in crime, both figuratively and in every since of the word. But that, too, is another story.

A week had passed, and while even the FBI was involved in catching my husband's murderer, the efforts of the authorities had been thus far, unsuccessful, and I was becoming annoyed. What I couldn't figure out though, was why the FBI was involved in a simple homicide? Well, according to the gentleman who handled the funeral arrangements for Malcolm's service, my beloved was still considered government property, and for those of you who don't know, you do not mess with what belongs to Uncle Sam. Ain't that something? Malcolm was a man, a human being, but in the eyes of our country, he was merely property... (shaking my head.) The authorities assured me that Damon would not get away, but I, on the other hand, was not so sure, and once again, the devil reared his ugly head. I convinced myself that I would do the work the law was supposed to do, so I took to the streets. I gathered from the people in the "hood", any information that I could, and when I was certain I had what I needed, I, with help from Jackie, devised a plan.

The authorities were doing everything in their power to catch Damon. They had alerted and set up stake-outs at the airports, train stations and bus terminals, and agents were stationed outside his grandmother's home, but still, there was no sign of him. They were looking in the wrong places and I knew this. In my mission to gather more "intel" on this man, I discovered where he was hanging out, but I would never tell.

Once the details of my *"Take Damon Out"* plan were complete, and just as Jackie and I were set to put it into motion, my mother came to me. Now, keep in mind, that she had no idea what I had been up to, or was plotting to do. At least, I didn't think she knew. She was not staying at the house with us so when the plans were discussed, she was not present, and whenever she was around, we were careful not to say anything. In fact, no one knew what was about to take place but Jackie, myself and God. Oh yeah, God... I have always joked that I could never get away with anything, because for some reason, God would always tell my mother what I was up to. I mean, I don't care where I was or what I was doing, she would always know. I can recall her telling the story of how when she dropped me off at school one day, God said to her, "In the front gate and out the back." I was ditching school. I wasn't stupid, I would make sure (like most of us who would cut class), to be home when I was supposed to, and of course, I intercepted the calls that came in from the attendance office, but none of that mattered. I still got caught, and all because God was a tattletale. (Just kidding Lord, many of those revelations, I am sure, saved my life.) Well, I don't know why I thought this situation would be any different. Out of the blue, she came to me one night and said, "I don't know what you're planning to do, but the kids have already lost their father, they cannot afford to lose their mother, too." The plot was spoiled. I listened to my mother, heeded the warning, and decided to let God, and the authorities, handle it. Dang!

A few days later, we held services for Malcolm and said our last goodbyes. It wasn't easy, but we got through it and shortly thereafter, just as they had promised, the authorities arrested Damon.

At his trial, Damon was sentenced to 30 years. Although the authorities assured me he would serve at least 90% of his time and that I would be contacted any time he came up for parole, he only did a total of sixteen-and-a-half of those years, instead of the twenty-seven he should have served for the murder of my husband. It was my oldest daughter, who, after doing some research, found out that he had been released. Surprisingly, I don't really know how I feel about it. I know I do not hate him, because I don't feel it in my heart. I guess you could say, in a sense that, perhaps, I have forgiven him. Would I be able to make the same claim if I saw him today? I'm not sure, I can only hope so.

Someone once asked me how, after such a devastating life experience, was I able to go on? My reply was simply, "For the children." What I didn't know at the time was that, this was the same response Jackie Kennedy had given when she was asked the very same question after losing her husband, John. Motherhood, there is no job more important. We do what we must, we find the strength. I was determined to live for my girls, to raise them as best I could. It's what Malcolm would have wanted and today, he, too, would be proud of the women they have become.

In the weeks that followed, I gathered my children and returned home to California. It was the place where I would pick up the pieces of my shattered life and move forward. Forward, without my beloved husband by my side. And while I knew it would not be easy and the road would be long, I knew my faith in God would see me through; it and my children were all I had.

Chapter Three
<u>Junior: Let Me Tell You About This Clown</u>

Fast-forward to the Year 1998. I had just moved back to Vista, California, in with my girl Stephanie, and once again, we partied! But this time around, things were a little different. We had grown some since our previous partying days in San Diego County and were now more responsible, working adults. The hustle however, was still very much alive in me, and my girlfriends. Some things never change.

Five years later, there were still times when I mourned the sudden and untimely death of Malcolm, especially on his birthday, our anniversary, and the anniversary date of his death. I may not have shed as many tears as before, but I would still get a little depressed and I always questioned what could have been and how did my life get here? As the years came and went, these moments of sadness became less frequent. I had learned to accept, and deal with, what had happened. And although the tears and the depression eventually went away, I still miss him.

In November of that same year, a new man came into my life. His name was Junior. Sigh. I must take a deep breath for this one because, it's funny, shocking, and draining, all at the same time. But this chapter will be, almost as brief as the marriage itself.

Junior was young, and I do mean young, and I wouldn't find out until later in the relationship, just how young he was. He was ten years my junior; instead of nine as he had previously told me. Big difference, right? Whatever the case may be, I did not like being lied to, and was not very happy when I found out his true age. But, he was exciting, hip, and handsome and he had great taste in clothes. I love a man that can dress. In fact, he was so cool, that a male friend of ours would refer to him as *Rico Suave.* We met at one of the clubs on base, and yes, he, too, was a marine. As time went on, we began to spend a lot of time together. He appeared to be nice enough and the kids seemed to like him, at first...

In that same month, Stephanie decided to move to Atlanta and gave me the option of keeping the place that we now shared. It had been almost thirty days since I'd met Junior, and right around that time I had a brilliant idea. I ran it by Stephanie and, of course, got the thumbs up.

You see, Junior had been complaining about how much Uncle Sam was taxing his wages. He needed to do something to keep more money in his pockets, so, of course, I suggested we get married. And, why not? He needed some dependents and I needed both medical and dental benefits for myself and the kids. Now, I guess you could say that what we had was a "Contract Marriage." This is a term used in the military when two people decide to get married simply for financial gain. However, we did genuinely care for one another (at least we did at the time), but it wasn't long before that changed. So, in December of that same year, we went to Las Vegas and became husband and wife. Shortly thereafter, Stephanie did relocate to Atlanta and Junior moved in permanently. It would be, unbeknownst to me at the time, the beginning of the end.

Things were going well, initially, that is, until this person who was all of five years older than my oldest child, tried to rule my girls with an iron hand. Whew! When I look back at things now and how they went down, he was lucky they didn't tie him up somewhere and beat the crap out of him. Of all the men I have ever dated, or married, I had never known my children to have such disdain for anyone as much as they did for him. However, as far as I was concerned, they were justified in their feelings. Let me explain.

He would wait until I was gone (to work

o r wherever), and then proceed to treat my girls like they were in the Marine Corps. He would shout orders like he was a drill sergeant talking to his recruits, and when I would get home, I'd get an ear full...from both sides. This man was all of five feet tall, maybe, and when he found that he could not bully the kids to get his way, he would get angry. I am telling you, it's hard to write this because, every time I think about it, I start laughing. This man was so short, I can recall him sitting in a chair and his feet not touching the floor. How did he ever think that with his age, size and nasty attitude that my children could view him as anything other than Grumpy Smurf?

I tried to comfort my children by telling them to just be patient, for you see, Junior had received new military orders and would be shipped off to Okinawa, Japan in January. Talk about your short-lived romances. Yes, ours truly was. Let me sum it up for you. We met in November, married in December and I put him on a plane to Okinawa in January. Once again, it was just my kids and me; the only difference was, I had a husband overseas. My kids were pleased with his departure, and I must admit, I enjoyed the peace that was restored in my home once he was gone.

The terms of the marriage were simple. Junior would receive extra money for having a wife and kids, and in return, we would receive all the benefits the military had to offer. I was working, so, I only required him to send money home if it were necessary. I have never been greedy, and I wanted to be fair, so, if he did as we agreed, I did not anticipate any problems. I could get health and dental checkups for my kids and myself, and he could pocket the extra money. Well, as you can probably imagine, things did not quite go as planned, and the money would soon come between us.

Understand that, with the military, it takes about 45

days before you start to receive dependent pay, so, I was not alarmed when, in February, I informed Junior that I needed him to send me a little something, and he, in turn, told me that he had not yet received the additional monies. You see, I also knew that he would receive back wages for the pay increase he was due, so, instead of having an allotment set up where the additional monies would come directly to me, I trusted he would do the right thing; per our agreement. When March rolled around and there still was no extra money, I smelled a rat. But, again, instead of pressing the issue, I gave him the benefit of the doubt and waited patiently. April came and when he tried to pull the same stunt again, I let him know, in no uncertain terms, that the jig was up and that I was hip to his game. I also reminded him, that I had been down this road before and knew how things worked. He told me that he would send something in a couple of weeks, and he did.

I received a check in the mail for about $600 but imagine my shock and surprise when I went to the bank to cash it and found out that he had stopped payment on the funds! Okay, I was through being nice, the gloves came off. If this was the road he wanted to travel, I had no problem going down that path with him, but what he didn't realize, is that, I was the one doing the driving.

I called and tried to explain to him that I would not stand for this and that the additional money he received did not even belong to him. Technically, it belonged to me and the kids and that, if I had to, I would go to his commanding officer and report him. He had violated our agreement. He then tried to convince me, in so many words, that they (meaning the military), would do nothing on my behalf and that the way things were handled during that time, had changed since the days when my former husband, Malcolm, had been in the Marine Corps.

Let me put a little bug in your ear ladies and gents. For those of you who don't know, the four-letter word "wife" carries a lot of weight with the military. I don't care which branch. And the one thing they will not tolerate from one of their own is the act of neglecting their responsibilities so, I don't know who this little boy thought he was talking to or dealing with, but clearly, he had no clue. Like I told him, I had been dealing with the military and its way of life for years. I mean, think about it. When I first became a military wife, he was still watching GI Joe on television and fantasizing about being a marine. He wasn't even old enough to vote so, how in the *H-E-double-hockey-sticks* did he think he could run game on me where Uncle Sam and MY money were concerned? Silly rabbit, tricks are for kids. They never learn (shaking my head). It was now almost May 1999, and I'd had enough!

The internet was just getting into full swing and

since I did not have a computer, I was not technologically savvy and really had no experience with the net, so, I enlisted the help of my intelligent, adolescent daughter. I guess Junior thought he was untouchable because he was in Japan, but I have never been a dummy, nor have I ever been slow. I grabbed my daughter and off to the base library we went. Once there, I instructed her to pull up the Marine Corps Base in Okinawa, Japan. I did not know the name of the base, nor was I certain of the unit Junior was in, but the good Lord must have been looking out for us once again because, when my daughter pulled up the list of officers in charge, their units, names and phone numbers were attached. We printed off the list and headed back home. That night, I picked a number at random and made a call. To my surprise and relief, I'd hit pay dirt. The first and only number I ever dialed was a direct line to Junior's unit and his Commanding Officer, Staff Sergeant Smith. I will never forget his name. Here we go, let's do this...

I explained to the Staff Sergeant what was going on, and he and I had a good laugh when he stated that the extra money Junior was receiving, was not his own. I informed him that I had already tried, in vain, to convey that very same thing to my husband, and that I knew the routine and what I was entitled to. The Staff Sergeant assured me that he would have a serious talk with my loving hubby and that he was certain Junior would do the right thing.

When the next pay period came around, I spoke to my spouse who promised that he would send another check, but nothing ever came so, I made another call to his commanding officer. After about four weeks of this madness, I had become increasingly impatient; not only with Junior, but with the Staff Sergeant as well. Nothing had changed, and despite all the promises from both Junior and the Staff Sergeant, I still had not received any form of payment. At this point, I decided that, if necessary, I would take this matter to the next level. I was done speaking with the Staff Sergeant regarding this situation.

A few days later, I dialed the number that I had been calling in the days and weeks prior. It was around lunch time over in Japan on this day, so I was not sure I'd even get anyone on the line. Well, not only did I get someone, but this time, it was Junior's Sergeant Major, and *she*, was a sister... Now, for those of you who don't understand how profound this statement is, let me take a moment to explain. The mere fact that this high-ranking official was not only a woman, but an African American Woman, a sister, meant Junior was in serious trouble. I can only imagine what some you who are reading this (especially those of you who are either active or retire duty) are thinking.

A short time after I'd finished running things down to this female officer and we ended our call, I received another call from guess who? When I answered my phone, Staff Sgt. Smith was on the other end of my line. He proceeded to tell me what they were going to force Junior to do since he would not comply with the previous directive.

When the Staff Sgt. laid out the details of what and how I would be paid, would you believe I objected? Now, do not get it twisted, I wanted what I was entitled to, but I informed him that I was not necessarily concerned about the back or previous month's pay, I just wanted Junior to start sending regular payments from that point forward. However, the Marine Corps would not hear of it. He stated that my husband would not only start sending the current payments but, he was also required to send the back pay that I was due, and that the payments would be made concurrently. In other words, the money I received every month would be doubled until all back support owed to me was paid. Did he screw himself or what? If he had just done right as I had asked, as we had previously agreed, he could have avoided all that trouble, but like most men, he thought he knew best. Well, now the joke was on him. I tried to warn *Mr. Thought He Was Untouchable*, but he wouldn't hear of it. I held the title of "wife", and that was all I needed. For a Lance Corporal in the Marine Corps to have to give up approximately $1200 per month of his pay, was a hit in the pocket that he could not afford. I mean, his actions defeated the whole purpose of him taking on dependents in the first place! Oh well! I laughed all the way to the bank; but the actions of this young idiot, just continued, and over time, proved to be more astonishing. I must say, he was persistent.

When his plan to try and keep me from getting what was rightfully mine to begin with backfired, he then tried to claim my children on his taxes. Yep, it just keeps getting better. This was one of the things to which we had agreed before he tried his little scheme, but of course, you know by now that I wasn't going to let that happen. In his pea-brain however, he had the audacity to think that those terms of our agreement were still in effect. I can only guess that he came to that rationalization because he was forced to pay me. What a schmuck. He called me a few weeks later to say, "You can go ahead and claim the kids, my tax return was kicked back." What he didn't know, was that I had already filed my taxes, claimed the kids, received my return, and spent the money. I ask you, who did he think he was dealing with? Really? As with most women, I was always one step ahead of him. My reply was simply, "Okay."

Shortly after that incident, Junior tried to have the lights in our apartment turned off. How did I know? I called the electric company one day to conduct some other business, and while doing so, I found out he had taken the account out of his name. What his smart behind didn't understand was that, because we lived in an apartment complex, they would not turn the lights off but simply remove his name from the account. No problem. Long story short, I took care of that, too. I found this truly amusing and thought by now that he would give up but, he had one more trick up his sleeve. He should have quit while he was ahead.

Around August of the same year, I received a court document in the mail. My "beloved" husband was filing for divorce. The document stated that it was not necessary for me to do anything, and since Florida was his legal state of residency and we had no children or property together, the marriage would be dissolved after 30 days. I said to myself out loud, "What? I don't think so! Negro we are in a lease together on this apartment until December 1st, and I will be doggone if you think you're getting off that easy." For some strange reason, he could not get it through that thick skull of his that he was not in control! I had the power, and before it was all said and done, he would recognize that.

I called the court where he filed, spoke to a clerk, gathered all the information I needed, and wrote a letter to the presiding judge. I explained the situation and all that had occurred over the past few months. I then requested that the divorce not be granted until the terms of the apartment lease had ended. About a week later, I received another notice in the mail from the same court clerk. The notice simply stated that our divorce would not be final until November 29th! Boom! Game ova...

I really hated to get ugly, but this young boy needed to be taught a lesson, and I could almost certainly guarantee that this would be one lesson he would not soon forget. I was a force to be reckoned with, and he should've asked somebody. Nevertheless, my work here was done, and I never heard from his lame behind again.

Over the next five or six years, I really focused on

myself and raising my children. Oh, I dated off-and-on, but nothing serious. During this time, my oldest had graduated college, it was the twins last year of high school, and mama was ready to make a move.

I had been preparing my children, since the twins were about three-years-old, for my departure and had often told them, that when the twins reached 18, I was leaving. Now, you might think it was cruel, but I had done my part and was convinced that I had raised them to be strong, independent women, and like eagles in a nest, it was time for them to fly. I knew they could, and would, survive, and I was always just a phone call away. The reality is, they were probably ready for me to go and to be on their own. So, in 2005, with the help of a relative, I made arrangements for them to move into their own apartment. Their rent was paid up for six months, they had enough household furnishings for two homes and I left them my car. Yep, I set them up; and with just the clothes on my back, I, like my friend Stephanie, moved to Atlanta, Georgia. And while my daughters may not have understood my decision at the time, I am proud to say that I was right, and survive they did. I can truly say that, God forbid, if I should drop dead today, I know, without a doubt, that my girls will be just fine.

Chapter Four
<u>William: More Tricks than Treats</u>

No one could have ever made me believe or even fathom that in 2011, at the age of 46, I'd be working a temp-job, sleeping on a friend's couch and struggling daily to hold it together. The economy was in a slump, and after supporting him for many years, even before the marriage, my husband of one year, William, decided he no longer wanted to be married! Okay, some of you may say I initiated it because I made the remark, "I think I want a divorce." But hadn't I said this before? It was no big deal then, so what was different this time? In fact, I never actually said it to him out loud; I'd sent him a message via text. So why was his response and his actions so different this time?

Could it be because I had ripped him a new one just a few days prior? I don't think so. When I got on his case, it was justifiable; at least, in my mind. I mean, when a man neglects what he is supposed to do for his family, how long do you let him continue to do so before you let him have it? Oh, don't get me wrong, while this behavior was not typical, it was frequent. We'd had this problem in the past and I would take the time to talk with him, explain my displeasure with his actions and we would come to an understanding, or so I thought. And like the other husbands before him, he, too, was forewarned that at some point, if certain behavior patterns continued, I would eventually lose my patience. Could this be the reason he so easily agreed to divorce? In the past, if I said, "I'm divorcing you" or "I want a divorce," he would ask why, and we'd have a good laugh about it. Not this time, this time was different.

The fact of the matter is, I truly believe, no, I know without a doubt, that he'd left the relationship long ago but was too much of a coward to just say so. It was only after that realization and the many attempts to save my marriage that his true feelings surfaced. In other words, my statement,

"I want a divorce" was what he had been feeling all along. How do I know? When I later asked him if he was ever going to tell me the truth about how he really felt, his reply was, "Eventually." Ain't that some...? Well, you know.

Angry? That's an understatement if I've ever heard one. Mad as hell? Yeah, that's more like it. I wanted to hurt him, no, KILL him, no, just make him wish he were dead. You know, kind of like how the husband in the movie, *Diary of a Mad Black Woman*, ended up? Helpless. But unlike the character in the movie, I, his wife, would have been the one to inflict pain on him. I had to remind myself daily, and I do mean daily, that he was not worth it, and that I am worth so much more. His loss? Hell yes, but at the time, those words meant nothing to me. In fact, one night I phoned him, and when he answered, I merely said, "I'm going to kill you." And I meant every word. I had every intention of doing just what I'd said. God help me.

Yes, even as Christians, we sometimes go through things and try to convince ourselves that the consequences are worth it. Okay, maybe I'm the only one. There was an inward battle going on and I found myself trying to reason with myself. *If you harm this man, you risk going to prison for the rest of your life! So, what else have I got to lose, except for my freedom, or maybe even my life? I can live with that and, who knows, maybe if I do it right, I can actually get away with it.* Yeah, I had not only tripped out but, I'd also fallen. Fallen into a downward spiral; I had to get a grip on myself. And it didn't help that on that weekend, I had been watching true life movies of women who had been scorned by the men who had promised to love them. Women who had succumbed to their anger and who had killed their husbands. Women like Betty Broderick and Clara Harris. Yep, my mind was playing tricks on me; the devil was having his way and winning the battle.

All I could really do at this point was pick up the pieces of my shattered life and move forward. But, how could I? Especially when the sorry bastard wouldn't even help pay for the divorce. Wow, I'd picked a real winner this time.

What I had to understand and come to grips with was, that we cannot control other people or their actions, and while I could not continue to beat myself up, understand, that it was William who I really wanted to harm. And, as much as I wanted to hurt him, even that would not have been an easy task, considering he weighed approximately 250 pounds, and I, a measly 113. As Adele Givens would say, "Sort of like a whale and a tic-tac." (For those of you who have seen her comedy routine, you will know exactly what I'm talking about, for those who have not, Google it, if you wish.)

In my lifetime, like many of you, I have been through

some things, but, I did not see this one coming; at least not to the point that he would come out fairing much better than me. Oh yes, the Negro got over like the fat rat he is. Hey, do I sound bitter? Okay, maybe just a little, but I had a right to be, at least I thought so. I mean, the man was sleeping under his own roof, in his own bed, (oh, I had a bed, too... at my mother's house!), driving his new vehicle, and enjoying the fruits of my labor. Things like most, if not all, of the household furnishings, and even the clothes he puts on every day; right on down to the towels he washed his stinking behind with, *I* had made it all possible!

Now, don't misunderstand me, he did bring some things to the table when we first met. He had some household furnishings of his own, a couple of cars, and a motorcycle. He was living in his own place and had not one, but two jobs. In fact, he was in better shape financially, than I was when we first met. Yeah, in the beginning, he seemed to have it all together. But, somewhere along the road we were traveling, he seemed to lose his ambition (or so I thought). And me, being the strong, supportive woman and sistah-girl that I am, was there to pick up the pieces and help him hold it together when his world fell apart. Funny how quickly he recovered when he wanted out.

He no longer needed me to hold him down, but you'd think the ungrateful, you-know-what, would have at least called to see if I was still breathing. Huh! The Negro even kept my dog that I paid real money for, because after the break up, I could not even afford to bring my beloved pooch home. Why? Because I didn't have a place to live, oh, and I no longer had a job, and have you seen what it costs to fly an animal across the country? My unemployment income was not that good.

I was just getting my credit back on the road to recovery when all of this went down, and you know, for some of us, that's a really big deal. Especially, when you can't blame your bad credit on the state of the economy in the first place, because your scores were already in the toilet prior to the recession. I mean, companies were so desperate to generate business, that they gave me two cars (in my own name) and a couple of credit cards. I had a decent job that I liked, was making good money and doing well for myself. Then, I did something really stupid. For the first time in my life, I let this so-called man, lead. Oh, he led me alright; right out of my stable job and decent life, into one of loneliness and despair.

Is that what God intended when He commanded the wife to be submissive to her husband? Oh, I am convinced that God has jokes, but this can't be what he meant. I was trying to walk in God's word and do as I had been taught, so when William wanted to leave our life in California behind, and relocate to Georgia, like a good wife who trusted her husband and believed he only had our best interest at heart, I followed him.

I've often wondered, and I still don't know, how some women do it. You know what I mean? They follow their husband's lead over and over, even when they know it isn't right. Guess that's why I'm where I am today. Maybe, just maybe, the husbands of the women who put up with certain behaviors are worth it. Clearly, mine was not. God knew this; and maybe God knew something else that I didn't. Maybe He knew that the outcome would have been different had I stayed and dealt with the situation a little while longer. Well, like I always say, I am not God, and I was not sticking around to find out. Sorry God. Oh, and I really wish some of those people who tried to talk me out of, first, the marriage, and then, relocating, would have tried a little harder. I wish they had told me in detail, what they saw or felt, instead of just saying, "You shouldn't" or, "I wouldn't."

Some didn't say anything at all, not until, after it was all said and done, and not until it was too late. Yeah, those are the people I really want to thank. Now, don't misunderstand me, I don't blame anyone but myself and William for what happened, but if I saw my sister, a loved one, or even a friend headed for disaster, I'd at least try to warn them. In the end, I probably wouldn't have listened anyway but, my point is, that some did not even try, and for those that did, they did not try hard enough. (I still love you though).

I blame him simply because he was not honest, and I blame myself, because I was stupid. I mean, how can you truly expect honesty from someone who is a Prozac-popping, almost two-cases-of-beer-a-day drinking, tobacco-chewing, manic depressive who doesn't communicate? Really? What the hell was I on? Nothing, and perhaps that was the problem. I mean, at least years ago and prior to this, when I was an addict, I didn't make such idiotic decisions. I don't even like men who chew tobacco. In fact, I didn't even like him when I met him, but I will tell you about that later. And I know it sounds hard to imagine or maybe even crazy, but believe me when I tell you, just as any of my friends or family members will, that during the stage in my life when I was a functional addict, a Negro had to put up or shut up. Hell, I had three kids and a habit to support, I didn't have time for foolishness and there was no room for compromise. And I don't care what you say, but maybe that was a part of the old me I should have kept. Not the drug usage, of course, but the attitude that came along with it. I mean, look where compromise and compassion had gotten me; broke, homeless, alone and sleeping on my friend's couch! And though I did not find it amusing, sometimes I had to laugh because I was mad. I wanted to hurt somebody (and we all know who that somebody was), but

I also found myself angry with the one person or being (if you prefer), that I never thought I would or could be for that matter; I was angry with God.

You see, I was not only attending church as I should when all of this occurred, but I had also rededicated my life to the Lord. So, how could He let one of His own, especially me, go through such things? But, did He really? Did God not send me warning signs and I ignored them? Of course, He did. All I know is that, at the time, at that precise moment, I was mad at Him. I truly believed in my heart that if I showed compassion, especially to someone with whom I had spent so many years of my life, God would intervene. Was I not truly in tune with God? I know, I know, I've heard it all before, *we should not be unequally yoked.* William wasn't even going to church, let alone trying to live saved. However, I had met and shared some significant years of my life with this man before I resumed my walk again with God, and had reasoned with myself, that if I'd turned and walked away from our relationship because of it, what would he think of God then? What kind of impact would it have had on him and any chance of him having his own relationship with God? Weren't we supposed to be an example? Wasn't it Jesus who said, "With love and kindness, I have drawn thee?" I was really confused, so I chose to stay.

In the midst of it all, I became frustrated, not only with God, but with the church and everything it represented, so, I basically walked away from it all. Oh, I still went to church off and on, but even as I was writing this, my walk was not the same. At this point, I was not only frustrated, but agitated and disgusted. I felt betrayed.

Looking back at my beautiful wedding, and a beautiful day it was, I should have run! I was marrying the devil and I knew it. Walking down the aisle, I began to cry, and while everyone else thought my tears were those of joy, I realized, that I was shedding tears of despair. *"Why am I doing this?"*, I found myself, asking myself, only to reason with myself. *"He's got some good qualities. No, he hasn't been stable on a job in four years, and yes, he owes the IRS $25,000. He doesn't think things through, he's not as affectionate as I'd like him to be, and he refuses to attend church with me as he promised, but so what? He is romantic, at times, in his own way. He loves me, and I feel safe with him."* But, how can you truly feel safe with someone who says he was sent to you from the gates of hell? Maybe I was unknowingly doing drugs; maybe he slipped me a mickey. For four years? Really? Naw, I don't think so, and I rationalized at the time that he was just joking about being from the gates of hell, but who in their right mind jokes about such things? The radical, heavy metal music he listened to, the graphic and gory animations and movies he watched, and let's not forget the Prozac, should all have been clues! Duh! Red flags all over the place!

This thing had affected me in more ways than one, and more than I cared to admit. And not just my livelihood, but me as a person. Self-esteem, shot, confidence, shot, he took everything, stripped it away; or, maybe it was my own doing. I cried like I never had before, hurt, pain, anger. And when I wasn't crying, I was thinking of ways to get even. Revenge! I know, "Vengeance is mine says the Lord," but sometimes, I think the Lord needs a little assistance.

At first, I would send nasty text messages. Yes, this Christian woman did. Cursing him out and damning him to hell, and when the coward refused to take my calls, it only angered me more. Then I started snooping, spying, invading his privacy, getting as much information, or dirt (depending on how you look at it), on him as I could. Why? Initially, I was going to use it against him in court, but then it became

toxic, obsessive, but as sick as I was; I soon discovered, just

how sick, he really was...

I found photos of young white women, (they were

over 18), but, in reality, they were mere girls. In these

photos, they were not only kissing each other, but they

seemed to be engaged in oral sex with each other as well, it

was hard to tell. All I know for sure is, that the photos made

me sick to my stomach and enraged me even more. He was

sicker in the head than I thought. He'd once told me that I

was only the 4th black woman he had ever dated, which I

thought was ironic, considering, he is almost as black as tar,

but it never dawned on me that his preference was anything

but black. Here again, reality slapped me in the face! That

discovery only fueled the fire in my search and destroy

mission, and while I will not go into details of what I did or

what tactics I used, let's just say that one of my tirades sent him shock waves in the pocket, to the tune of almost $800! Hell, hath no fury...

I can hear you all say, "You're not the first to go through this, Jesus, and others for that matter, suffered a lot more than you." Well, I'm not those other people. I'm talking about me, and my name is not Jesus. When someone is hurting, they don't want or need to hear those words, and had I been Jesus, I'd have sent him straight to hell!

Oh, I had my good days when everything seemed to be going just fine, and then... all hell would break loose! On one day in particular, while at work, I decided to check my Facebook Page, which I did periodically every day, and there it was, staring back at me, taunting me. My former employer's son had posted a message which said the company had moved into a larger facility. This could only have meant that even in this unstable economy, business for them was good. Now you may be asking, "So what does this have to do with the story?" Well to answer your question, a hell of a lot!

This was the place where I had been employed for over two years, and in that time, I had climbed the ranks and proven myself worthy to hold the position I had secured. You know, the position I gave up when I left California to follow what's-his-name? All the hurt, humiliation and anger returned, and the flood gates of my eyes, which had been so calm just days prior to this, opened again. All I could think about was where I would have been, the money I gave up and could have made and the stability I had. It was all gone... and again, the devil raised his ugly head. Depression set in, the thoughts of death and revenge returned and flooded my mind. I somehow managed to finish out the day at my "temp job", (humph, temp job), gathered my things and went home... to my friend's couch!

The more I thought about it, the more my mind played tricks on me until it won, and it was on this night that I made the call to my then-estranged husband and threatened to kill him. I did not even bother to wait for a response from him, I hung up immediately. I wanted him to understand just what I was feeling and know just how serious I was; and I was, dead serious. (No pun intended). What I didn't know was that, not only was I in shock, but I had experienced what I would classify as a nervous breakdown, and the only way to stop the pain, was to see him never take another breath.

Yes, at that point, I was willing to sacrifice myself to see him in death. Was I tripping? Perhaps losing my mind? Maybe I was, but what you must understand, is that I felt as if all the life had been zapped out of me. I was going through the motions of my daily routine, but I was not alive, and I refused to die this death alone, so I was taking him with me.

His mother would be hurt, and his daughter, devastated. So, what! I did not care and why should I? They didn't care about me. Serves them right; and at least his daughter would collect survivor's benefits over the next four years. All I cared about, was how I was feeling. I laugh as I remember my mother saying how glad she was when our breakup occurred that I was in California and he was in Atlanta; but what she didn't know, was that I was planning to return to the great state of Georgia.

When I wasn't concentrating on how I could enact revenge, or carry out my murderous intentions on William, I was contemplating suicide. I cannot honestly express to you, even as I write this, the weight of the shame I carried. I would be driving down the road and, quite often, I would have to talk myself out of driving off a cliff, or a freeway overpass. Then there were days when I would think to myself, *just take some pills, lie down, go to sleep, and never wake up; at least the pain would stop.* But then, God would remind me of my beautiful children and grandchildren. How would they feel? Would they understand, or would they resent me for being such a coward and taking the easy way out? I thought about how hurt they'd be, about all that we had been through and survived together, and I just could not do that to them. Once again, God used my children to strengthen me. Praises to His name! And who knows? The way things were going for me at the time, it would have been just my luck to end up either disfigured or brain-dead, so, I decided to suck it up and keep on living. I told myself, *this too shall pass.*

I guess you're wondering how it got to this point? Humph, you tell me, because I have asked myself that very same question. Let me take you back to the beginning of this stage of my life, of how and where I encountered this man. And unlike chapter two, which was difficult to write, recalling the events of this chapter was just the opposite. I was mad as hell, and it, (Chapter 4), would become not only the easiest to write, but the catalyst for the book itself.

As you recall from the previous chapter, my girl Stephanie had relocated to Atlanta and, after numerous visits with her, in 2005, I decided to move there as well. I had already been on the dating scene in Georgia for about two years prior to making the final move, nothing serious though, I was just having fun and enjoying life. Then in March of 2006, I met him, William. It's a funny story how we came to be, because initially, I wanted nothing to do with him. In fact, my girls and I were out for a night and minding our own business when he came along...

My friends and I had been invited to an old-school-night spot, where the admission and watered-down drinks were free, by the president of one of the local motorcycle clubs. We were celebrating the birthday of one of our girlfriends from Detroit, and I had broken up with a man I had been dating, just hours before. Yeah, you heard right. It was March, and he was the second man I had dated since arriving in Atlanta, and I was convinced that they were all nuts! That night, I had just, both literally and figuratively, walked out of that relationship, so the last thing on my mind was another; I should have followed my first mind… hindsight.

The men in Atlanta were either gay or on the DL (Down Low), and those that were straight, or heterosexual, were just crazy, and after the last two I had encountered, I'd decided I wanted no parts of any of them. Seriously, I can personally recall how, just about every other week, on any given day between 2006 and 2008, some nut had killed his female companion, then would proceed to climb the tallest building he could find and threaten to kill himself. And who can forget the Atlanta courtroom incident; where several people, including a judge, were shot and either wounded or killed? Yep, crazy I tell you. So, when Mr. Smooth (William) walked into the club that night, I ignored him.

Make no mistake, he was my type; big, black, and bald, and he seemed nice enough, but I was not at all interested. I guess you're probably saying, "It seems like all of the men she's written about, were her type." Well, while it is true that I didn't usually discriminate when it came to dating men, when it came to their physical characteristics, the ones that William possessed, were my preference. He was definitely my flavor!

We had waited so long for his arrival, (we wanted to go to another club) that I became annoyed and verbally stated as much. I remember saying, "Who is this nigga (keep in mind for those of you who find the use of this word offensive, that I am being transparent and relaying events and thoughts as they actually happened), where is he and why are we waiting on him? Is he the president of the motorcycle club?" Yes, I was annoyed, so I purposely did not even give him a second glance when he finally entered the room.

As William proceeded to introduce himself to our small circle of friends, he let it be known that he did not shake hands with women, and he greeted each one of us with a hug. However, when he got to me, he lifted me in his arms and embraced me. All I thought was, *Wow, here we go again. Another nigga who thinks I am so cute and tiny that he can put me in his pocket.* Again, I was annoyed. It has been said that he literally swept me off my feet, but had I truly known what was in store, I'd have turned at once and ran in the opposite direction.

Once all the pleasantries were out of the way, the entire group headed for the door so that we could get to the next spot. William asked me to ride with him, of course, but, I declined and rode with my girls. I'm telling you, I was not even vaguely interested in the man, but my girls, being the 'hustlers' they were, encouraged me to at least see what he was about. I mean, it was obvious he was trying to get to know me. They tried to entice me with their words. "Girl, he is sexy," one of them stated, "And he is driving a black sports car," said another, "And he has two jobs." Ding, ding, ding. Okay, now I was curious, but not enough to entertain the thought of getting to know him.

When we finally arrived at the other club, I made sure to get a good look at this nice sports car I'd heard about. It was a Grand Prix! Nice, but still a Grand Prix. *Big deal*, I thought to myself; goes to show how much my girls knew. Once inside the club, William behaved as most men do when they are trying to impress you. He bought us, especially me, whatever we wanted and was the perfect gentleman. We ate and drank to our hearts' content, and partied like rock stars until it was time to go. Funny, I can't recall if I even danced with him.

Anyway, after we closed-down the club, someone came up with the bright idea that we should all go to breakfast. I don't know who I should thank for that, but if I had to guess I would say it was one of the fellas. Man, was I ever going to get away from this guy? But hey, I was always down for a good meal, especially when someone else was paying. Might as well ride this one out.

We actually had a nice time; good food, conversation and laughter, and a couple of hours later, it was time to depart. It just so happened that all my girlfriends lived on the same side of town as the restaurant, as did most of the guys, but as fate would have it, both William and I, lived in the opposite direction. In fact, he had to go past the area in which I lived to get to his own home. I bet you can guess

125

how this turns out. It was decided, that since my home was in the direct path that William would be traveling, he would be the one to drive me home. He was probably thinking, *Great, I finally get her alone*, while I, on the other hand, was thinking, *oh great, he's finally going to get me alone*. Same thought, different reaction. The ride home was pleasant, and we continued to have some decent dialect, so when we arrived at my place and he asked for my number, I obliged and gave it to him.

In the days and months to come, William pursued me constantly; he was very attentive. We spoke regularly, almost daily, and started to hang out together quite often. You know how it is when things are fresh and new. Did it bother me that he was still married to his first wife? Naw, they had been separated for at least eight years and, besides, I had not planned on this thing going any further.

Being that he was a member of the motorcycle

community, most of our outings were centered around the activities and events sponsored by the various motorcycle clubs. There were parties, lots of parties; but we also participated in charity functions, community picnics, and of course, weekend rides. It was a brother and sisterhood, and I enjoyed what they were doing. In fact, I enjoyed it so much, that eventually, I, too, joined the motorcycle set. I must admit, I was intrigued by the seemingly gentle giant. In his club, he was referred to as the General, and people on the set seemed to hold him in high regard. They respected him so, not only did my fascination for him intensify, but my attraction to him as well.

We took trips together. He was the first person to introduce me to "Black Bike Weekend" in Myrtle Beach, South Carolina. It was during this trip, and to his surprise, that I questioned if we were a couple? He was startled and wanted to know why I would ask such a thing? I explained to him, that I had been listening to the Michael Baisden Radio Show in the days prior to our trip, and it was said that men and women need to establish if they are in a relationship, and if so, they need to clarify that relationship. It was also said that just because you are spending time with someone, doesn't mean that it is anything more than just two people hanging out, and that women too often mistakenly think otherwise. They, meaning the women in these scenarios, tend to think that the man is feeling the same way they are, and end up with their feelings hurt when they find out otherwise. Oh, I paid attention, and I was not about to fall victim to that, not after what I had already been through with the last two clowns I'd met in Atlanta, and especially since this statement came from a man. I needed clarity and stated as much to William. His reply was, of course, "Yes, we are a couple." I knew that our connection was not purely physical, but I had to hear him say it. So, it was on this day that we, as far as I was concerned, officially became a couple, exclusive and monogamous. We were so inseparable that you would hardly ever see one of us without the other, especially when we hit the M/C (Motorcycle) set and we were, believe it or not, the envy of many.

In July of that same year, William went to his childhood home in the city of Detroit, Michigan, to see his mother. It was a trip he and his only child, a daughter, took every year. I missed him terribly, and evidently, he missed me just as much because a few days later, he asked me to join him. Yes, I was going to meet his family. This was getting serious, and very quickly, and I knew from that moment that this was more than just a causal relationship. William was not, is not, the kind of man who does such things on the fly. He was winning my heart.

Shortly after our return from Michigan, my home became a volatile, and almost an unbearable, place to live. After the break-up with fool number two (the guy I'd left on the night I met William), I moved back in with fool number one, the first man I had been involved with in Atlanta prior to my relocation in 2005 and when I finally settled there. It was only temporary and strictly a roommate situation. However, he came in one night drunk, talking crazy, as he often did, and woke me. It was midnight and I had to be up for work at 5am. I'd had enough of this foolishness and although my own place would not be ready for another three weeks, I could not deal with the madness any longer. I decided I would go stay with my girlfriend Stephanie until my rental unit became available. After only two hours of sleep, I got up and headed out to work.

William called me later that day, as he often did, and I started venting. I told him what was going on (he knew the whole situation, I had been forthcoming and honest with him) and that I was going to find some place to stay for just a few short weeks. In that moment, he let me know just how much I really meant to him. Without hesitation or question, he opened his home to me. I resided with William for three weeks until my townhome was ready for move-in, and while I had vowed that I would never again live with a man who wasn't my husband, this too, would soon change.

William and I lived quite a distance from each other; I lived in Riverdale and him, in Lawrenceville. For those of you who are not familiar with Atlanta suburbs, let me tell you, we were in no way within close proximity of one another but, despite the 45-mile drive (each way), we spent a lot of time together, which usually occurred at my place. At first it was just weekend visits. You know the routine; William would usually come by on Friday, stay until Sunday and, on occasion, I would make the trip to his home. However, since most of the happenings in the M/C Community were on the weekends and in my neck of the woods, it was just easier and made more sense to hang out at my place.

As time went on, the weekend visits became more like extended stays, and before I realized what was happening, William began to spend more time at my home and less at his own. This was not a problem for me, I thoroughly enjoyed having him there and, being a single woman in a strange place, it felt safe to have him around. In fact, during the times when he was away, which was usually when he had to work additional hours on the weekend or after we'd had a misunderstanding, I did not sleep well. So, it did not come as a complete surprise to me, when he practically moved in.

Over the next few months, we spent every moment

we could together, and, in July of the following year, I moved in with William. Now, this was not a rash decision, nor was it easy for me. My landlord had decided to sell the townhome where I was living and, since William and I were together all the time anyway, it just made sense. I didn't have to worry about looking for, nor finding, another place to live; it would be financially beneficial to the both of us, so I moved to Lawrenceville. His place was nice, nothing spectacular, but it was in a good area (an area nicer that the one I'd just left), and I was quite comfortable there.

It was also during this time that William's career began to take a turn for the worst. One of the restaurants where he worked was struggling and he was laid off. A couple of months later, the other restaurant where he worked, experienced some changes in management and William was not happy. He had been with this establishment for ten years and was promised part ownership, but when management took on a new partner, things changed, and he quit.

I, on the other hand, was doing very well career wise. I had been with my employer for about four months when I was promoted, and with that, came an increase in salary. So, while William, who was now collecting unemployment, was trying to figure out his next move, I assured him that we would be fine. *I* would hold us down. A short time later, William decided he wanted to go into business for himself. He, unbeknownst to me, had been researching extensively, and while doing so, in his infinite wisdom, decided to become the owner of his own big rig. He would follow in the footsteps of his father and become a truck driver. But there was one problem; he had never driven a big rig in his life. His unemployment benefits were running out and he had to do something fast, so he went to truck driving school. After about a year, it became evident to both of us that the trucking industry was not at all like it used to be. Gone were the days of making lucrative money while hauling loads. Things had changed drastically, and if you were an owner/operator, which William was, they were even worse.

For those of you who have no idea what I am talking about, let me explain. Being an owner/operator of your own 18-wheeler versus being an employee of a trucking company, is supposed to give you more flexibility and the opportunity to make vast amounts of money. If you cannot purchase your own truck outright, you lease it, and just like an automobile, at the end of the lease, the truck is yours. Sounded good to me, so I trusted that William knew what he was getting us into. (There's that word again, trust) ... It would later become crystal clear to both of us that this was probably one of the worst decisions during our time together that he could have ever made.

As an owner/operator, and unlike a driver who is employed and regulated by a company, you assume *all* the responsibilities that come with that leased vehicle. And by responsibilities, I mean, any, and all repairs, fuel, insurance, and the biggest expense of all, the monthly lease payments of course.

If the truck does not run, you don't make money, and that goes for all drivers whether they own the truck or not. So, for the owner/operator, that means all expenses are still his or her responsibility and come out of the driver's pocket, weekly, regardless if they make the money to cover those expenses or not. Yes, I said weekly! The lease payment of $450, or more, plus the insurance and everything else that went along with the maintenance and upkeep of the vehicle was deducted, even when my husband didn't make a dime! I cannot tell you how many times William's paycheck said, "Net Pay: $0.00." Through it all, I stood by him, and over time, he would often say he was done with trucking. Whenever he was sure he no longer wanted anything to do with the world of trucking, William would come home to find a job in the restaurant business, only to end up returning to the trucking industry a few weeks later. This went on, believe it or not, just about the entire time we were together, and still, I stayed; supporting him and holding us down. Did it bother me, his flipping back and forth? Of course, but I understood his struggle and instead of ridiculing him, I encouraged him to keep trying; as any good woman should...I guess.

In the following year, the company I was working for shut down, and while I was able to secure another job rather quickly, I was not happy. I decided that since I hated this new job and William was hardly ever home, (he had been gone out on the truck for at least six months) it was time to make a move. I was tired of being by myself in

Georgia so, in April of 2008, I quit my job and returned home to California.

I had been back home and out of work for just a little over a month when, in May, I landed a new job. This was the job that I would later come to know as my "dream job." You know, the one I mentioned previously, the one I left for William? I moved out of my mother's house in San Bernardino, and back once again to San Diego County. Yes, I was back, right where my heart longed to be. I stayed with a girlfriend for about thirty days, then moved into a new place and set up shop for myself and William. He was still out on the road, sometimes making money and sometimes not. Oh, don't get me wrong, whenever he had a good run, the money was more than adequate, but most times, he didn't have much to contribute. But time marched on and we, as a couple, did the same.

Around August of 2009, William came off the road

for what I thought was the last time and joined me in California. At this point, it didn't bother me so much that he wanted off the truck again. We had been down this road so much that I almost expected it and, to tell you the truth, I wanted him home with me. It was also around this time that my walk with God intensified. I had given my life completely back to Him a few years prior, and it was during this time that I refused to waiver or be persuaded otherwise.

Now you may find this next part hard to believe, and frankly it really doesn't matter if you believe it or not, but I can tell you from my own personal experience that a man and woman, who are in a relationship, *can* cohabitate without being sexual. Yes, William and I lived more like roommates than lovers, which was fine with me since I was trying to maintain my walk with the Lord. But, I must admit, that at times, it bothered me, and I found it odd, that he didn't try to make a move on me. However, at the end of the day, his actions, or lack thereof, made my path to righteousness an easier one.

The fact that I had chosen to rededicate my life to Christ was never an issue for us, but what would surface and cause some minor grief, was William's refusal to attend church with me (as mentioned prior) except for special services. By September, William's divorce from his first wife was finalized and we set a wedding date for the end of May of the following year.

Prior to the wedding, William did find a job closer to home, however, after just a few months, once again, he became restless. He was discouraged by the fact that he was not making as much money as he thought he should have been. And while it was true that when he calculated the costs of the gas it took to get to work and the hours he spent commuting back and forth, the expenses far outweighed what he was bringing home. But still, we needed the money, and all I could think was, *here we go again.* During a discussion about this latest plight, I encouraged him to remain with the business (he was back in the restaurant industry), and while doing so, continue to look for work elsewhere, perhaps, something closer to home. I also reminded him that we had a wedding to pay for. He agreed, and that was the last I'd heard of it, but to my surprise, it would not be the end of it.

Our wedding day came and went, and while the ceremony was beautiful and the reception all that I could ask for, I found it strange, that even on this night, we did not consummate the marriage. Was it because I'd had too much champagne and fell asleep? This was probably not the case at all, he just wasn't interested. I found this a little odd, and if this was the case, what was it (the marriage) all for? I tried not to dwell on it and, when I questioned William about his actions, he simply apologized. Perhaps he was just tired...I guess.

We had both taken a week off from our jobs so that we could have some sort of honeymoon. It was our desire to go out of town, but financially, it just was not in the cards. We were still paying for the wedding, so we decided to make the best of it and stayed local. We hung out and just enjoyed one another's company. It was nice, but when the honeymoon was over, and it was time to go back to work, William hit me with yet another blow. He refused to go back to his job!!! I could not believe what I was hearing. What in the world was going on with this man who, when I met him, had his stuff together and, on some level, helped provide for me when I couldn't provide for myself? That man was gone!

He had made the decision, without my knowledge, to quit his job. Was he crazy? Hell, was I? In the three years prior to this, I insisted that he stop taking the Prozac. Evidently that was a mistake, because now, he was irrational and all over the place. Hell, he was making me crazy. Too tired to argue the point anymore and feeling defeated, I simply said, "Okay, find another job." Can someone get *me* some Prozac or Zoloft? Shoot, I felt like I was in the twilight zone! But being the dedicated sister that I am, I supported him, (humph) both emotionally and financially, and I still wasn't getting any! But, I had married him and had to accept what I had signed up for, and, what I didn't realize at the time, was that all the changes in his behavior, were probably side effects of quitting the antidepressants cold turkey. I was in a catch 22. It was not good for him to continue taking the drugs but, it seemed that since he'd stopped, things had gotten worse. Once again, hindsight is twenty, twenty.

In mid-June, and after having no luck of finding

another restaurant gig, an impatient William decided (yep, you guessed it), that going back into trucking was his only option. This decision, however, would require us to relocate back to Georgia (sigh). Somebody please stop this rollercoaster, so I can get off!

After toiling with this latest development, I went into the office where I worked and informed my boss of the pending move. The following month, we moved out of our home, I rented a room and William went back on the road. And wouldn't you know it? Just three weeks later, he got a call about another restaurant job. Too late. So, on September 21st, 2010, I said goodbye to my family, friends and coworkers, and with William and our dog, loaded up our belongings and began the long drive back to Atlanta.

Prior to our departure, I had been looking for employment and had set up an interview for the week following our planned arrival. William had already secured a home for us, which brought some relief to the anxiety I was feeling, and I had to give him credit for at least helping to make the transition a smooth one.

Things were going well. I secured the gig, was making the same salary I'd been making prior to leaving California, and we had finally settled into our new home. Then, in November, it happened again. William wanted off the truck! He was an-over the-road driver on the east coast and hated driving in the bad weather conditions. I blew a gasket! I didn't care what his reasons were, he knew before winter set in and before he took the job, that this was par for the course! We could have stayed in California! Why in the hell did I leave my friends, family and most importantly, my cushy job? I was fed up with this back-and-forth, indecisive crap and I put my foot down. I let him know that, in no uncertain terms, this was the very last time I would deal with this and he'd better be doggone sure that this was what he wanted. I felt like I was talking to a child and I am sure he did, too, but wasn't he behaving as a child? I was done letting him decide his own fate, and rightfully so, because every time he made one of these rash decisions, it affected me too, in one way or another. Let the man continue to lead? How could I, when he had no idea in which direction to go? In December, William came off the road to share with me, what would be, a home for the very last time.

In January of 2011, William landed a new job in a new restaurant, but this time was different. It was a sports bar-and-grill, his area of expertise, and he was in charge. The new owners had no idea how to get the operation up and running and were grateful, or so it seemed, to have him. The compensation was good, (he was finally making a little more than I was) and he had free will to do as he pleased. He was finally content, thank God! But as fate would have it, things took another unexpected turn.

While things seem to be picking up for us and finally heading in the direction in which we were both pleased, in February of that same year, just a month after my husband landed his new position, I lost my job! I was devastated. What part of the game was this? *Alright Rene*, I thought to myself, *you've been here before. Shake it off, get back out there and find something else. Besides, your husband is home and doing very well. Couple this with what you're bringing home in unemployment compensation, and you are still doing okay.*

I decided I would concentrate on finishing school. I mean, why was I worried? The roles had reversed; William was now able to do what he should have been doing all along and what he was doing when we first met, be the provider. So, while I was content and had finally settled into my new role as "homemaker" and student, I continued to casually search for a new employment. While there was no sense of urgency to obtain a new position outside of our home, my contentment would be short-lived, which is not surprising when you are used to being the bread-winner. So, in August of the same year and after not being able to find work, I made the decision to return to the west coast, where I was sure I could secure work rather quickly. Yes, in August of 2011, I headed back to California. We had only been married a year and were having some major problems. My departure was the beginning of the end.

I had only been back in California for a couple of weeks when the knock-down, drag-out, mentioned in the beginning of this chapter, occurred. William and I separated. This time, for good.

THE TRINITY

Chapter Five
Me, Myself and God

It has now been four years since the fallout of my last marriage, and while I must admit it has not been an easy road to travel, it has truly been an eye-opening experience. In February of 2013, I finally acquired my own place to live, and although I had only been able to secure temporary or contract work at the time, and the money I earned did not even come close to what I had become accustomed to, the work had been somewhat steady and constant.

Oh, there were times when I had to visit the local food banks and accept jobs that only paid ten dollars per hour just to stay in the workforce, but I learned that there is no shame in that, I had to press. And while I lived in a subsidized housing unit and at times I made more than ten dollars per hour, but still less than twenty-five thousand per year, I survived. God continued to make a way for me.

In March of the same year, I had to file bankruptcy and, in the process, surrender the last vehicle I'd had in my possession, but God was still faithful. During this time, He blessed me with a job that was within three blocks of my home, and just as God promised, just as he did for his faithful servant Job, He began to restore to me everything I'd lost. It brings tears to my eyes to even think about it.

I had only been in my new place for "seven" months when I received a notice to move. The number seven. I have heard about, read and researched its meaning from a biblical standpoint, but it did not dawn on me until just now, how significant it had become in my own life. Those of you who are biblical scholars already know, that scripture states, the number "seven" represents completion and/or perfection. Watch how God worked.

I lived in a high-rise studio apartment on the fifth

floor. The building had been sold and the new owners wanted to renovate, so, to make the changes they wanted, I had to move. At the time this occurred, I was not offered any alternative dwelling and, just like that, was simply told to get out! I had sixty days to secure a new place to live and while I was not certain about where I would go, I was not worried. I had prayed about it, and I trusted God. My neighbors and I acted quickly to preserve our homes. It was September 2013.

A couple of weeks later, I received another notice from the apartment management team. It seemed that rather than displacing the residents, (which of course included me), they were willing to work with us and try to come to some resolution. However, at the time, they did not state what that resolution might be, and while some of the residents who immediately became alarmed jumped ship and left, I remained steadfast. I was no longer angry with God and had renewed my faith and my trust in Him, and I knew, somehow, some way, everything would be fine. It was in HIS hands.

By this time, I had also been without a vehicle since July. If you recall, God had already blessed me with a job within walking distance of my home, so getting to work was no big deal, but when the bad weather rolled in, walking the three blocks to work would become somewhat of a challenge. So, when God also blessed me with some new people in my life (my co-workers), they offered to drive me to and from work. He was *still* working it all out...

In February of 2014, "seven" months after I'd lost my own transportation, he blessed me with another vehicle. And let me be quick to point out that it was not just any old car, he gave me what I asked for. My new ride was a definite upgrade in comparison to the one I'd lost. It was bigger, better and my payments were a lot less. A couple of weeks after purchasing my SUV, and around the end of February, I lost my temporary job. But, again, I wasn't worried. I had a roof over my head (at least for the time being), and transportation, so I could find a new job. I knew that I would probably receive unemployment compensation (which I did) and with that, I could pay my rent, car note and maintain my livelihood. But, God was not done!

Two weeks later, on March 15, 2014, exactly "seven" months after I received the initial notice to vacate my residence, I got the keys to my new place! And get this, I moved within the same apartment complex to a bigger unit, and my rent was $130 less per month than what I had paid for the studio! DOUBLE FOR MY TROUBLE!!!

Through all of this, I have been humbled. My eyes

were opened, and I learned that is it not *I* who's in control, it is God who holds all power. He has taught me that it's okay to ask for help and that sometimes, He must break you down so that He can build you up, and for that, I thank Him. I have come to appreciate things that others don't even think about. My home is peaceful, tranquil, and it provides serenity for me.

No longer am I bitter about my failed marriages and no longer do I want to kill my former spouse, now, I pray for him. And when the anger tries to rise and get the best of me, I am able to shake it off. I have forgiven him, and, myself. I have truly grown from this whole ordeal. Where there was once hurt, there is now peace. The shame I once carried has been replaced by joy and my faith in God, restored. I no longer question why I went through what I did; I just know that I had to. It was a necessary process.

Perhaps, it was because of my own past behavior, of how I had treated others, or maybe, it was just because.

And although, in my heart, I knew from where my blessings flowed, what came from my lips said just the opposite. In other words, be careful what comes out of your mouth.

In my last marriage (and I'm sure other past relationships) I was quick to use the word *I* when it came to my blessings. *I* made it all possible, *I* held it together, *I, I, I*, never stopping to give thought to what I was saying or doing. When God "Opened My Eyes", I realized that I had been taking the glory away from HIM and attributing it to myself (talk about revelation).

Whatever the reason, this journey has helped in my growth toward becoming the woman I should be; the woman whom GOD has intended me to be. And while I still have a long way to go, I know, without a doubt, that my future is much brighter than I could have ever imagined.

At the completion of this writing, I have graduated college and obtained a Bachelor's Degree in Business. I have also secured a permanent job position which pays almost as much as I was making before any of this started, and God is still opening doors. Whether it is an awesome career move or ownership of my very own company, I am looking forward to what the Master has in store for my life.

Oh, and, I guess you're probably wondering if I will ever marry again? Only God knows for sure. If it is in His plan for my life, of course I will, but for now, I am cool with just doing me. But what I can tell you is this, there are some stipulations that must be met before I would even consider settling down again. The main and most important thing being, that before the next man can ever convince me that he truly loves me, he _must_ love God First.

When I Opened My Eyes

Who is this staring back at me?

How did I get here, how can this be?

Looking in the mirror, I see a smile,

The pain has been erased,

There is now sunshine in a once dark and lonely place.

The Happiness has returned, I am at peace, I am free,

When I opened my eyes, I saw a brand new me…

-Rene

Epilogue: Still Have Questions?

What was Malcolm's family's' reaction toward Rene upon hearing about his death?

What caused the argument that led to the ultimate breakup of Rene and William?

How has Rene's life been since the writing of this book?

Did she every remarry?

The answers to your questions can be found in "When I Opened My Eyes, the Limited Edition"

Available December 2018

Made in the USA
Columbia, SC
13 February 2025

53806526R00089